Ira Sankey
Singing the Gospel

IRA SANKEY
SINGING THE GOSPEL

Kelley Deegan Bruss

journeyforth®

Greenville, South Carolina

Library of Congress Cataloging-in Publication Data
Bruss, Kelley S., 1975–
   Ira Sankey : singing the Gospel / Kelley S. Bruss.
     p. cm.
   Includes bibliographical references.
   ISBN 978–1–60682–107–7 (perfect bound pbk. : alk. paper)
   1. Sankey, Ira David, 1840–1908. 2. Composers—Biography. 3. Hymn
writers—Biography. 4. Singers—Biography. 5. Gospel musicians—
Biography. I. Title.
   ML410.S176B78 2010
   264'.23092—dc22
   [B]
                                        2010023115

Illustrations by Paula Cheadle
Design and page layout by Craig Oesterling

© 2010 by BJU Press
Greenville, South Carolina 29614
JourneyForth Books is a division of BJU Press

Printed in the United States of America

ISBN 978-1-60682-107-7

15 14 13 12 11 10 9 8 7 6 5 4 3 2 1

FOR MY MOM,
WHO HAS BEEN SINGING THE GOSPEL TO ME
SINCE THE DAY I WAS BORN

CONTENTS

Prologue—October 1871

"Nearer and Nearer Comes the Breakers' Roar"

An hour after falling asleep, Ira awoke to the sound of waves slapping near his feet. He rolled his overcoat into a bundle and sat up, surveying the shore and the city. Above the shelter his trunk had provided, he felt the wind still blowing strong. It pushed hissing flames northward, burning more of Chicago each minute. The sun rising over the lake seemed only an extension of the fire's glow.

Ira was desperately thirsty. He stood and rolled his head side to side, wincing at the aches inflicted by his brief rest and the long night's efforts. Then he crouched by the water. He flicked at the surface to clear away ash and debris. He tried for a moment to rinse soot from his hands, then gave up and ran them, wet, through his hair. He would have to keep looking for water fit to drink.

Ira pushed his belongings beyond the lake's reach and began to walk along the shore. He passed many piles— family portraits and heirloom clocks, leaning against bags of clothes and boxes of food. And he passed many filthy people, most too busy with their own plans for survival to make eye contact. When he saw some rowboats tied to a small dock, he felt a rush of hope.

"Can I take one of these out where the water's clean?" he called to a man nearby.

"If you think you can handle one on that water, take it," the man said. "No one's boating for pleasure here any time soon."

Lake Michigan churned under the same winds that stoked the fires, but Ira was strong. He rowed near to his piled up possessions, pulled the boat onto the beach, and loaded up the trunk and bundles. Then he pointed the bow away from the city and began to row again. He moved under the railroad tracks, held above the water on massive pilings. Out farther he went, beyond the worst of the fire's filth. Then he leaned over, cupped his hands, and drank wildly, ignoring the water that slid down his sleeves and chin. The boat pitched as he leaned toward the lake, and he reached back with one hand to steady it and himself, panting as he did.

His thirst satisfied, Ira grasped the oars again and rowed toward a partially constructed breakwater. He tied the boat and climbed out onto the new wall. All day he watched fire devour the city, his home for many months. The sound of explosions traveled through the smoke and out across the water. Bands of men were blowing up buildings, forming a line of rubble to stop the fire from spreading farther south.

The sun began to set as it had come up, one flame among many. Ira shivered, and then recalled the words he'd sung days before: "Dark is the night, and cold the wind is blowing, nearer and nearer comes the breakers' roar; where shall I go, or whither fly for refuge? Hide me, my Father, till the storm is o'er."

"Father in heaven, I'm out here," he prayed. "I know You see me. Help me. Keep me from these waves. Save me from the fire. Please, please bring me back to my family."

Ira decided it was time to return to the city. The fire was moving north, leaving behind smoldering ruins—and perhaps a way out. He eased back into the rowboat. At first the churning water carried him away from land. But he strained against its pull and finally reached the shore.

The lakeside swarmed with people. Some, like Ira, were returning from the water, venturing back to see what remained where their homes had been. Others huddled close to their bundles and boxes with a wary eye for the looters and thieves who had already done a full night's evil work. Still others stood ready to turn the city's trouble to profit. Among these, Ira found a drayman with a cart.

"Can you find the unburned end of the Fort Wayne and Chicago Railway?" he said.

"For ten dollars I can," the man told him.

"You get me there, sir, and I'll give you ten dollars gladly," Ira said.

The streets were littered with hot bricks and twisted masses of telegraph wire. There was smoldering rubble too. The searing air had carried debris to the water, but much remained behind in piles that smoked and burned still.

Somewhere a clock tolled 3 a.m. Ira registered the three bells but was unable to collect his thoughts enough to determine how long he'd been awake. Something gentle hit his face. He wore bits of ash all over, but this was something different. Something wet. Rain.

It hissed and steamed as it fell on scattered fires. Ira welcomed the new sounds, so much more hopeful than the roar of the flames.

The drayman got Ira to the railroad station, where they unloaded his things together. Ira bought a ticket and checked his belongings. Heedless of his grimy appearance, he sat down in a restaurant and ate. Only as he finished did he realize how hungry he'd been. His last meal had been on Sunday night. Now it was early Tuesday morning. The train wouldn't leave for at least an hour. Ira took a final swallow of coffee, and then surrendered his seat to another diner with exhausted eyes and began to walk. He knew where he was going: Madison Street, the block between La Salle and Clark, the last place he had seen Moody. They had been together Sunday night, there at Farwell Hall, when the fire broke out.

Ira's feet carried him forward while his mind took him back to that night. He had been singing "Today the Savior Calls." The words seemed prophetic now: "Today the Savior calls: for refuge fly; the storm of justice falls, and death is nigh." There had been bells, the same warnings they had heard over and over those last weeks.

Farwell Hall was only blocks from the courthouse. The latter building's great bell sounded the city's general alarm when the fires were most threatening. An editorial in Sunday morning's *Tribune* had warned that citizens were becoming dull to the alarms. It reminded them to heed the bells.

That night, as Ira had reached the third verse of his song, the clatter of fire engines joined the bells. The people had grown restless, and the meeting ended abruptly. Moody and Ira had parted outside the hall.

Ira stood now at the very spot. Farwell Hall was gone. Every building that once stood around it was gone. A partial wall stood here, a lonely chimney there. Filthy people stepped gingerly through the rubble, reaching down now and again to pull out something that seemed salvageable.

Ira looked for a long while, then turned back for the railway.

As the train began to carry him home to Pennsylvania, he watched out a window. The whole country seemed to be on fire. He rested his head against the glass pane. The smoke carried with it his hopes. Chicago was done. His work there was done. He would go back to his family and, with luck, the job he'd left a few months before. This chance to do more had been only a fleeting dream.

Ira closed his eyes and sleep came at last.

1

"Tell His Love and Sing His Praise"

Ira struck the tuning fork firmly, and the note rang out soft but clear. Then his voice came, stronger, easily heard into the corners of the choir loft.

"Do! Sol! Mi! Do!" he sang.

The choir members joined him, each section finding its part for the opening hymn. Ira directed the slightest break in sound and then brought them into the song.

"A mighty fortress is our God, a bulwark never failing; our helper He, amid the flood of mortal ills prevailing."

The choir sang the entire first verse, and then Ira turned to the congregation and waved broadly. Shoe leather scraped against the floor, and wooden benches groaned as the people stood. Voices swelled, filling the room to the roof.

Ira led song after song. Some he regretted by the end, when tight harmony grew loose and notes slid flat. But most of them filled both his ears and his heart with pleasure.

He had learned the joy of music as a boy at home. David and Mary Sankey loved songs and passed that love to their children in the most natural way—by singing with them. On winter nights when the dark came early,

Ira and his brothers and sisters would sit around the fire, following their mother's lead in century-old hymns. David Sankey, a businessman and state legislator, traveled frequently. But when he was home, his splendid bass rumbled near the bottom of each song. Ira and the others learned to sing parts as small children, bringing home the tunes they'd learned at church and pairing them with complementary hymn texts.

Ira remembered his mother kneeling by his bed many nights. The songs changed, but the routine was almost always the same.

"Close your eyes, Ira."

"One more song, Mama?"

"Sweet boy, I'm all sung out."

"Please? Just until I fall asleep."

She laughed, a sound he loved almost as much as her singing.

"No, certainly not until you fall asleep. No doubt you'd have me sitting on this floor all night."

His wide-open eyes gleamed with the reflection of firelight from the sitting room. He didn't beg, but she spoke again as if he had.

"All right. One more. Just one, though, and you must close your eyes."

Her voice was clear and full, lower than most people expected.

"Hush, my dear, lie still and slumber, holy angels guard thy bed."

Ira knew all four of Isaac Watts's verses. But he was silent as his mother sang.

"May'st thou learn to know and fear Him, love and serve Him all thy days; then to dwell forever near Him, tell His love and sing His praise."

She paused, then sang again the last phrase, more slowly: "Tell His love and sing His praise."

She stood, letting her hand slide across his quilt and off the bed.

"Good night, Ira. God grant you rest."

He wouldn't open his eyes until she was gone and the door shut out all but a sliver of light upon the floor. The song would remain in his ears, as if she were standing there still. And he would mouth the words with her voice in his head, tapping a finger on his stomach with each note.

Ira learned to read music at home too, following along in a book as the family sang. He quickly memorized beloved tunes such as St. Martin's, Belmont, and Coronation, perhaps best known for its pairing with the text "All Hail the Pow'r of Jesus' Name."

Now, at eighteen, he stood before the choir of the Methodist Episcopal Church in New Castle and passed along his love. Often in rehearsals that meant stopping a piece midword.

"Friends, will you sing that again so I may understand you?"

He asked it so frequently most choir members could frame the question for him and predict when he would ask it.

"I know," he said. "I know I am repetitive. But in singing our Savior's praise, I think our meaning must be clear if we hope to urge others to join us."

Ira's demands didn't hurt his rising popularity with the choir members or the church. He was soon asked to become Sunday school superintendent, on top of his musical duties.

Weekdays he worked at the bank where his father was president. But music was never far from his mind.

One afternoon he knocked on David Sankey's office door.

"Come in."

"Father, do you have a minute?"

"Yes, Ira. Close the door. Come," he said, gesturing at the chair nearest his own.

Ira stood instead.

"Would you sing a C, Father?" he said.

"What?"

"A C, middle C. Would you sing it, please?"

"Ira, what is this about?"

"It's about an organ, Father. We need help to sing well. We need it for the choir; we need it for the congregation. I need it. I want to know if you, or perhaps the bank, might make the necessary donation."

"Ira, we've sung in church without an organ for years, for many years, for forever, really. The music is wonderful. You've made great strides with the choir. You've even got them in their seats on time."

He laughed at himself, but his son did not join him.

"Father, I'm in earnest. We need this. The tuning fork works to give me my note. It's fine. My voice works to give the choir their notes. It's fine. But you hear how we stray. It's ghastly. And it's simply not necessary. A small organ, in the corner, hardly in sight, would bring everyone in beautifully and keep us where we ought to be."

David Sankey looked at his son. Ira's dark hair waved, despite his daily efforts to smooth it against his head. He dressed meticulously and worked that way too. David was not surprised to hear him arguing for musical precision as well.

"Son, please, sit down," he said.

Ira did.

"This is a question of much more than money, Ira," he said. "I will not address it as if you were still a boy. Your mother and I raised you to enjoy music as a gift from God, a gift that blesses us and honors Him. We count musical instruments as part of that gift, but many of our friends do not, Ira. They suspect that worship with an instrument becomes mere performance. And that is not a concern lightly brushed aside, son."

"Father, I think—"

"Listen to me, Ira. What you consider a beneficial addition, others call an open door for worldliness, even wickedness."

"Yes, Father, I know, but is there no chance of talking to them? Explaining to them? Perhaps they don't understand how we'd use it, or even what it sounds like."

"Just lead them in joyful noise for the Lord, son. The organ may have its day in the church, but this is not that day."

Ira returned to his own small desk. He straightened his papers and prepared his pen for copying. His eyes and fingers seemed willing to work on their own, leaving his mind free to sing.

It was music that had drawn Ira into church. When he was a child in Edinburg, Pennsylvania, the Sankeys belonged to a congregation that worshipped several miles from their home. Ira walked the route faithfully, regardless of which family members joined him. He didn't yet crave to know God, but he wouldn't dream of missing an opportunity to sing with a group.

When he was sixteen, Ira walked to The King's Chapel, another church near his home. He went there for the music that surely would be part of the scheduled revival meetings. But this time he left with more than a song in his head. The message pierced his heart with a deep conviction of his own sinfulness. He tried to push the thoughts away, even making light of what he'd heard. But a man from the church pursued Ira and urged him to make a decision for Christ. Until then, God's grace had been merely a subject nicely set to pleasant tunes. But Ira could no longer resist the knowledge of his own sinfulness and his desperate need for that grace.

In 1857, the Sankeys moved about six miles east to New Castle, where Ira's father was assuming presidency of a bank. After Ira finished high school in New Castle, he took a job at the same bank. But his heart wasn't in the world of finance. Ira loved his duties at the church. As Sunday school superintendent, he urged the other teachers to include the direct words of the Bible in their lessons as much as possible. His own classes were always well-attended— and he took his own advice, frequently quoting or reading lengthy passages of Scripture.

Through his work with the choir, Ira was gaining a reputation beyond the boundaries of New Castle. He began to receive invitations to sing at revival meetings, conventions, and conferences of all kinds, even political gatherings. He generally accepted with pleasure, enjoying the opportunities to travel, to learn, and, most of all, to sing.

The only time he came close to formal musical instruction was as a young man, shortly after he'd begun his work at the New Castle church.

His teacher was William Bradbury, a man in his midforties then and well-known both inside and outside the music world as a composer, director, teacher, and even, for a while, piano maker. Bradbury was determined to bring musical instruction into the mainstream, paving the way for the children in Sunday school as well as in public schools to be taught how to sing. Bradbury believed teaching children to sing also meant providing them with songs they could sing easily and enjoy.

He composed the tunes for hymns such as "The Solid Rock," "Sweet Hour of Prayer," and "He Leadeth Me"— more than eight hundred in all. He also wrote the music for the first song many children learn: "Jesus Loves Me."

When Ira heard Bradbury would be in Farmington, Ohio, just fifty miles from New Castle, he knew he had to go.

Bradbury's sessions were short on the stories and jokes that others might have used to relax the class. He was a stern but passionate teacher.

"Talk little, sing much," he advised the choir directors in one session. It was advice he followed himself.

Ira soaked up lectures on sight reading, harmony, and effective approaches to teaching music. And with the others he sang and sang and sang—during classes and in services and at two concerts held at the close of the convention.

Then he went home, humming new tunes, and more focused on his music than ever. While David Sankey loved music himself, he was growing weary of his son's enthusiasm.

"I'm afraid that boy will never amount to anything," David Sankey said to his wife. "All he does is run about the country with a hymnbook under his arm."

"Better a hymnbook under his arm than a whisky bottle in his pocket," she replied.

2

"There's No Place Like Home"

Ira devoured newspapers from the time he learned to read. He wanted to know the issues of the day and learn what other people were thinking about them.

In early 1861, there was plenty to read and think about in papers across the country. South Carolina voted to secede from the Union on December 20, 1860. Other states followed as the new year dawned.

Ira observed with both interest and sadness as the thirty-three states appeared to be losing the ties that had bound them for nearly ninety years.

Once, his brother Charles brought home a week-old Cincinnati paper.

"Secession is anarchy," he read. "If any minority has the right to break up the Government at pleasure because they have not had their way, there is an end of all government."

Charles threw the paper onto the table.

"Read the rest," he said.

Ira scanned the piece, nodding.

"No doubt it's against the law," he said.

"Well? And what will be next?" Charles asked, not waiting for his brother's answer. "War. War, Ira."

"I believe they'll find a way out of this yet," Ira said. "There are so many proposals, so many ideas for a compromise."

"And which of them will please our southern brothers?" Charles said. "You have read their work too, Ira. You know as well as I they will not back down now."

In February the Confederacy chose Jefferson Davis as its provisional president until elections could be held that fall. The next month, Abraham Lincoln delivered his inaugural address as the sixteenth president of the United States. He made clear his intentions to preserve the Union.

But the first rumblings of the war that would divide the country had already begun. The day after his inauguration, Lincoln was informed of the desperate need for supplies at Fort Sumter, on an island just off the South Carolina coast. Union troops occupied the fort, though the Confederacy had been waging a political battle over its right to the property.

The needs at the fort pressed Lincoln to make a decision—accede to the wishes of the Confederacy and withdraw or force Union ships into the harbor with supplies, essentially starting a war.

After a month of advice from all sides—debate, headaches, and sleepless nights—Lincoln sent word to South Carolina's governor that the Union was planning to reach Fort Sumter with provisions only, no additional men or ammunition.

The Confederates fired on the fort April 12, before the attempt was made to bring in the supplies. Two days later, the American flag came down and the Confederate flag was raised over Sumter.

On April 15, 1861, Lincoln asked for seventy-five thousand volunteers to serve ninety days and put a stop to the rebellion, "to maintain the honor, the integrity, and the existence of our National Union." Patriotic fervor in the North was at a fever pitch after Sumter. Governors had to ask the War Department to increase the number of troops that could come from their states—they couldn't hold the boys back.

Ira and Charles Sankey were among the first in New Castle to sign up for service.

They joined Pennsylvania's Twelfth Regiment, Company H. Within days they were on their way south to Pittsburgh and then east to Harrisburg, the capital, where the regiment was mustered into the service of the United States.

They took the Northern Central railroad to Camp Scott, about twenty-five miles south of Harrisburg. For three weeks they drilled, turning the muddy ground into inches-deep sludge as they marched over and over it.

Ira sat beside a fire in mid-May, using a twig to scrape dried mud from his boots. He sang while he worked.

"Mid pleasures and palaces though I may roam, be it ever so humble, there's no place like home."

Ira started low, barely more than a hum with his lips moving. But he ended strong because other voices had joined his.

"Home! Home! Sweet, sweet home! There's no place like home. There's no place like home."

"Sankey, start another," said Bill Sharp, a good, strong tenor and already a friend.

"Just a minute," Ira said, shaving vigorously at a clump on his left boot.

Sharp found a twig of his own and threw it at Ira.

"Leave it alone, Sweet Sankey, no ladies to impress here, and your mama wouldn't mind her boy getting just a little dirty. Come on, we need a song."

Ira sighed as the others laughed. Then he smiled too.

"All right, Bill, I think a round of 'Nelly Bly' might not hurt."

Ira gave the note, and they started a rousing verse, then stopped almost immediately when their sergeant stepped into the circle.

"Sir!"

"Sit, men. I've got good news; at least I think you'll think so. We move out tomorrow."

He waited, smiling, for the whooping to quiet down.

"Now I don't know that you'll find it a vast improvement from our fun here in the mud, but we have a job to do. The rebs, as you know, have been hard at work knocking down our bridges. Well, we've got them rebuilt between Harrisburg and Baltimore. But we've got an idea Johnny may be looking for some more fun at their expense. We'll be relieving the First Pennsylvania and guarding the stretch."

Maryland had not seceded with the other slave states. It was, in fact, bitterly divided in itself. Baltimore in particular was a city on the brink of eruption. In a skirmish there between Union soldiers and a mob, four soldiers and twelve civilians were killed.

The mayor and the chief of police ordered the destruction of the bridges on railroads coming in from Philadelphia and Harrisburg. They were determined to keep more Union troops out of their city. Furthermore, by destroying train lines and telegraph lines, they were cutting off the nation's capital, which lay still further south, from the rest of the Union.

But a New York regiment finally pushed into Washington, D. C., and others soon followed, moving into positions along the railroads and immediately beginning work to rebuild the bridges.

Train service between Harrisburg and Baltimore re-opened May 9. Now two weeks later, Ira's regiment would take over the job of keeping it open.

There was plenty of singing that morning as the men broke camp and prepared to move into positions south along the railroad. They marched toward action with lighter steps than they had taken in weeks of drilling.

But the new work had much of the same tedium as their first weeks in the service. The men were organized for guard duty and worked shift after quiet shift, always watching for, but never seeing, the enemy.

When Ira wasn't on duty or sleeping, he was often singing. He and several other men helped lead songs for the religious services held in the camp. Soon Ira was organizing a small choir. The men sang for their own enjoyment as well as for the camp services.

The other soldiers praised them roundly, but most of the singers assumed they were good only in comparison to no entertainment at all. So the note came as a surprise.

"Sankey, you're part of that singing group, aren't you?" Captain Leasure asked.

"Yes, sir."

"Well, here you go. If you want to oblige them, it's fine with me."

The captain walked away and Ira looked at the paper he'd been handed. It was addressed to the "officer of the company with the men who sing so nicely on Sunday afternoons."

He unfolded it.

Sir, would your men be willing to join us some evening if their time allows? We have heard their singing from a distance and would like to enjoy it more easily. We would be

*honored by their presence and would
be glad if they would share some
small refreshments with us as well.*

Several families had signed their names below. At the bottom of the page there were simple directions for finding one of their homes and the words: "Sunday, 5 p.m.?"

To Ira, the Marylanders were Southerners despite the fact their state was officially neutral. But the people were divided. True, many were committed to their Southern brothers, but just as many were loyal to the Union. And a good many were torn, like their state, and trying to live above the rising fray.

Ira and a dozen other men from his regiment were at the appointed house just before five on Sunday. They filed in and followed the host's outstretched arm into a spacious room. Several ladies were seated in chairs along the walls, and as many men stood near their sides or backs.

"Thank you for coming, gentleman. If you know 'At the Cross,' it's a favorite here."

Most of the men nodded and looked to Ira. He gave a low note, and they began to sing.

"Alas! and did my Savior bleed? And did my Sov'reign die? Would He devote that sacred head for such a worm as I?"

The room was silent as they finished the first stanza.

"Would you join us on the last?" Ira said.

The sound of thirteen men had already filled the room. Now the volume spilled out, making its way back to the nearby camp as the afternoon singing had first made its way to the house.

"But drops of grief can ne'er repay the debt of love I owe: Here, Lord, I give myself away, 'tis all that I can do."

Later, over coffee and warm cornmeal cakes with maple syrup, Ira chatted with the host, who, he'd learned, led the choir at a local church. Only as he walked back to camp that night did he realize it was the first time in weeks he'd had a meaningful conversation that included no mention of politics.

That Sunday night sing was the first of several, and Ira wrote to his family that he and the other men always were treated with courtesy and kindness, not to mention outright enthusiasm for their singing. While there was music, the war seemed far away.

It seemed far away on guard duty too. The regiment didn't see any action while stationed between the state line and Baltimore. In fact, the men never even saw the enemy. The fears that the railroad would be retaken never materialized.

The history of the regiment later called the service "noiseless and inglorious . . . but highly useful."

The regiment was mustered out of service quietly, a stark contrast from the hoopla of three months past. It was quickly becoming clear that the ninety days the men signed for would not begin to suffice for the opposition building in the South. Many members of the Twelfth Pennsylvania went on to serve elsewhere in the war.

But for Ira, this was the end. His father had a new job and needed Ira's assistance. His employer was the government. His boss was Abraham Lincoln.

3

"Showers of Blessing Thou Art Scattering Full and Free"

When Ira finished his three months in the Army, he considered reenlisting. But many friends and family members urged him to come home. It was becoming clear that this war would not be a quick or painless effort. Families were just beginning to understand the danger their boys were heading toward. Ira considered the advice everyone offered, but it was his father's influence that held the greatest sway.

Ira came from a line of powerful leaders. His grandfather, Ezekiel Sankey, was one of the first settlers in the western part of Pennsylvania that eventually became Lawrence County. Ezekiel was a farmer and church leader and, eventually, a county sheriff.

His son Ezekiel Jr.—Ira's uncle—had his hand in businesses ranging from hotels to canal boats to railroads. He was a major during the Civil War. Ira's cousin Charles, the second Ezekiel's oldest son, also served in the war before turning to a career as a railroad agent. Like Ira, Charles was known for a rich, sweet singing voice. In fact some preferred his singing to that of his better-known cousin, who was heard at events around the county and the state.

David Sankey was eighth of the elder Ezekiel's nine children. He was only four when his father died. Like his older siblings, David learned early how to work hard and pursue on his own the education his mother couldn't provide for so many children. When he was fifteen, David took an apprenticeship to learn tanning and currying. At twenty he became a Christian and an active member of the church he had attended since childhood. David married Ira's mother, Mary Leeper, in 1830. Ira was the fifth of their eleven children. Two of his brothers died as infants and two others before they were ten, making Ira the first of David's sons to reach adulthood.

While Ira was still small, his father began to take progressively more prominent public roles. He served four years as a justice of the peace and then as a magistrate. When Ira was three, his father was elected to the Pennsylvania House of Representatives. Four years later, he was elected a state senator.

While in the Senate, just before Ira turned ten, David Sankey fought for passage of a bill that earned him the title "Father of Lawrence County." For more than five decades, men had argued for a new county adjacent to Mercer and Beaver counties. But representatives of the other two counties had opposed the change. David Sankey helped convince his colleagues in the Senate that the territory had sufficient people and resources to demand independent status. Twenty-five years later, a history of the county cited David Sankey's "untiring and persevering efforts" in bringing the measure to a "victorious consummation."

This was the man who argued in 1861 for Ira to leave the Army and return to New Castle when his three months were up. Not surprisingly, Ira did so.

In 1862 David Sankey accepted a federal job and took Ira into his new office. War was an expensive enterprise, and the Union was coming up short. President Lincoln and Congress created a position called commissioner of Internal Revenue and authorized collection of the first income taxes to finance the war.

David Sankey was appointed collector for the 24th Congressional District. Ira's job in his father's tax office—and the federal paycheck that came with it—freed him to pursue a developing interest in his life.

Ira had met Fanny Edwards shortly after his family moved to New Castle. Their fathers knew each other even before that. John Edwards, too, served in the Pennsylvania House of Representatives.

Fanny, two years older than Ira, was already a member of the choir when Ira became its leader. She was drawn immediately to his passion for music and for the choir's vital role in church worship. But Ira was too busy to notice her those first years of their acquaintance.

During the day, he labored over numbers and books at the bank. In the evenings, he read voraciously, preparing for Sunday school lessons or teaching himself songs that he'd later bring to the choir.

His Sunday school classes were always popular. Though it had been just a few years since he'd taken Christ as his Savior, Ira had grown up hearing the Bible and knew it well. He led a group of about seventy each week. They assembled to study the Bible together, discuss what they were learning, and receive counsel and encouragement. Knowing he would be before them every Sunday drove Ira to study as he never had before.

So it wasn't until those quiet war-time nights in Maryland, when home seemed so far away and danger so near, that he found himself with time to think of a certain choir member back home. When his Army service was done, he came home still thinking about her.

Mary Sankey watched one Sunday morning as Ira smoothed his beard for the third time.

"She doesn't love you for being particular, you know," she said.

"What's that, Mother?"

"She doesn't love you for your careful whiskers or your neat coat or brushed hat," she said.

Ira heard her the second time, but he was in no hurry to turn and face her. His mother spoke again.

"Well now, I'm not saying she'd want you all ruffled and mussed, but you needn't worry so much, Ira. Fanny isn't a girl so concerned with those things. She'd rather you have a careful heart and a well-tended mind."

"Fanny? I don't know what you're talking about, Mother."

"Indeed? Then I took you for smarter than you are," she said. "I expected you to know your own heart and to recognize when another is offered to you."

Ira turned then.

"When I know that heart is really mine, I'll tell you first, Mother," he said, kissing her lightly on the forehead on his way out the door. "Perhaps I'll have something to tell soon."

Ira and Fanny were married in September, 1863. Their son Harry was born in 1865. Ira continued to work with his father in the Internal Revenue office during the day. In the evenings, he and Fanny studied music together. Weekends, they traveled throughout Ohio and Pennsylvania where Ira was in growing demand as a singer.

Ira always had been convinced of the importance of music in worship. But his work with the choir helped him refine his ideas on the subject. He expected the choir members to hold themselves to the highest standards of character and behavior, reminding them they were representatives of Christ and of their church. And he verged on obsession in demanding they sing words more and more clearly.

"Ladies and gentleman, we cannot be efficient witnesses for Christ if no one understands what we are singing. Please, let us try that chorus again: 'He leadeth me, He leadeth me! By His own hand He leadeth me! His faithful follower I would be, for by His hand He leadeth me.' "

Ira devoured hymnbooks. He loved learning new songs and tunes and sharing them with the choir and then the church. In *Golden Shower of Sunday School Melodies,* published in 1862, Ira found a new piece by William Bradbury, the man who had given Ira his only taste of musical instruction.

"Lord, I hear of showers of blessing Thou art scattering full and free; showers, the thirsty land refreshing; let some drops now fall on me, even me, even me, let some drops now fall on me."

It was called "Even Me," and Ira liked the progression of the seven verses, especially the middle ones, pleading with the Father, Savior, and Spirit.

"Pass me not, O God, my Father, sinful though my heart may be; thou mightst leave me, but the rather let thy mercy light on me, even me, even me, let thy mercy light on me.

"Pass me not, O gracious Savior, let me live and cling to Thee; I am longing for Thy favor; whilst Thou'rt calling, O call me, even me, even me, whilst thou'rt calling, O call me.

"Pass me not, O mighty Spirit! Thou canst make the blind to see; witnesser of Jesus' merit, speak the word of power to me, even me, even me, speak the word of power to me."

Speaking the word of power was a decent description of Ira's own technique. There always was a tune. But the emphasis on diction over melodic expression was a hallmark of his style.

His drive and attention to detail weren't restricted to musical pursuits. In fact they contributed to leadership roles throughout his life.

In 1867 he was among the men who helped establish the New Castle Young Men's Christian Association, or YMCA. It was one branch of a growing nationwide organization committed to promoting spiritual and mental improvement for young men. Ira was elected the group's first secretary and eventually served as its president, presiding over meetings in a rented room.

As with other responsibilities, Ira threw himself into his YMCA work and found it to be highly rewarding. But he couldn't have known it was leading him to a meeting that would change his life forever.

4

"Sinners Plunged Beneath That Flood Lose All Their Guilty Stains"

Ira had been a leader in the New Castle YMCA from its birth. He was an obvious choice when it came time to appoint delegates for the International Convention of the Association, to be held that year, 1870, in Indianapolis.

"You know Moody will be there," he told Fanny.

"Yes. Be still," she said, holding a pin in her mouth and pinching the fabric at the shoulder of his new coat.

It was nearly impossible to read a religious journal those days without seeing some mention of Dwight Moody of Chicago. Moody was a shoe-salesman-turned-evangelist who shook much of his city out of spiritual lethargy with his energetic and successful efforts at establishing a Sunday school. Even in the school's early days, he organized as many as sixty teachers for more than six hundred and fifty students a week. He had given up his sales work and for a decade now had been a full-time missionary to Chicago.

"I do wonder whether the reality of him will hold up to what I have read," Ira said, careful not to move anything other than his mouth. "The man's preaching is said to be vastly removed from what we're used to hearing."

"I imagine you'll enjoy his stories as much as others do," Fanny said. "There. Now slip it off carefully so

"I beg your pardon," Ira said. "Give it up? Why must I give it up?"

Moody spoke in a tone that sounded used to being obeyed.

"Because I have been looking for you and needing you these past eight years. You must come to Chicago and join me in the work there."

Moody took a half breath, allowing the slightest moment for a response, but when Ira could not find his tongue, the other man continued.

"Music is the burden of my meetings," Moody said. "I am not fit to do it myself, so I must depend on others to lead the song service and start a tune at the end of my talks. Try to imagine how things fall apart when some inexperienced, though goodhearted, soul starts a song that's unfit for the day's message. Or worse, calls for a long-meter text and a short-meter tune. Everything is thrown to the wind and every person is wholly distracted.

"You, sir, do not have these struggles. It's clear you're a man who knows the value of a well-chosen song sung at the right moment. So you see, I do need you. I have needed you for some time. And now I have found you."

Ira hardly knew how to answer this stranger.

"I cannot simply leave my work and uproot my family," he said, a bit irritated at Moody's boldness.

"You must," Moody said. "You must, Mr. Sankey. I have need of you, but what's important is that God has need of you."

It was a tricky statement to argue against, so Ira chose not to attempt it.

"Thank you, Mr. Moody, sir, for the invitation. I shall think on it," he said.

And he would think of it. But he doubted his thoughts would be in favor of going.

Moody was not quite satisfied.

"Will you pray about it?" he asked.

"Yes, of course."

"Will you pray now? Right now? Here, with me?"

Feeling obliged and wishing to be polite, Ira agreed. Moody drew him aside to two chairs, and Ira found himself wondering how long this would take.

It was a moment.

"Father, your wisdom is infinite, your provision unmatchable. Your work is our privilege, your yoke our delight. Show me what I must do, strengthen me to do it. And Father, I ask the same for Mr. Sankey. Amen."

"Amen."

Ira spoke quietly, but his heartbeat seemed so loud and quick it must surely be noticed by those around him. They shook hands, and Moody left without another word for his plan or of a future meeting.

McMillan had stepped aside when Moody and Ira sat to pray. Now he hurried back.

"Well? Will you do it? What an opportunity for you, Ira! Surely this meeting was of the Lord."

Ira shook his head. McMillan seemed to understand that he wasn't saying "no," but simply that he was too bewildered for any better response.

Alone in his hotel room, Ira listened to a church bell peal the hour. Morning services were beginning, but he remained motionless on a chair by his window. He thought of Fanny and of Harry and Eddie on her lap. He missed them now as if he had been gone four years, not four days.

How could he ask her to leave her family and all that was familiar and move to the edge of the frontier? But could he ask himself to leave her there and go alone?

And what of his father? How would David Sankey advise the son he had called home from the war for a job at his side?

But to sing. To sing every day. To draw people to their Lord with a message carried on a tune. To work constantly beside Moody, that bold, rumpled man, and share with him the rich pleasures of rescuing lost souls.

Ira lay down on the springy hotel bed and closed his eyes.

5

"And Shall I Fear to Own His Cause"

The convention was drawing to a close when Ira received a note.

> Mr. Sankey,
> Would you meet me tonight, at 6 o'clock, at the corner of Michigan and Capitol? I would like to speak to the men as they walk home from work.
>
> D. Moody

Ira, McMillan, and several other Lawrence County delegates were at the corner when the hour turned. Moody walked toward them a minute later.

He didn't stop to speak or even greet them, though he nodded as he passed by. They watched him scan the sidewalk, then place a large crate in a central spot that would require passersby to move to one side or the other to continue.

"Mr. Sankey," Moody said. "Please."

He gestured to the box.

"Will you sing?"

Ira stepped onto the crate and looked down at Moody.

"Anything?" he asked.

"I rely on your good judgment," Moody said.

The other Pennsylvania men watched, some smiling, others with looks of astonishment.

Ira began to sing.

"Am I a soldier of the cross, a foll'wer of the Lamb?" The streets had not seemed particularly full. But as Ira's voice swelled—"and shall I fear to own His cause"— men gathered, curious, interested, compelled to hear the next verse in that powerful voice.

He sang four verses, then Moody was on the crate before Ira was fully off it.

"Gentlemen, you have little need of my words. My friend Mr. Sankey has just given you all the sermon you could ask for. 'Is this vile world a friend to grace?' Brothers, your hearts know the answer. And saints 'shall conquer, though they die.' Do you not crave that everlasting comfort? You have been soldiers, many of you. You have faced foes. Are you equipped for your greatest foe?"

The silence on that street corner was unnatural. Men held dinner pails still at their sides. They pushed their hats back and mopped sweat from their brows. The June sun blazed even as it began to descend.

Moody spoke for nearly half an hour, and then closed with a sentence that was more like an opening.

"And what does it mean to be His soldier? Will you join us in the Opera House, friends? Come with us, and we will speak further of the Savior and His righteous demands of our service."

Then he was off the crate as quickly as he'd stepped onto it. He sought Ira in the crowd near the front.

"Will you lead us to the assembly, Mr. Sankey? With a song, if you please, something familiar so the men may join in."

Ira and his Pennsylvania colleagues moved through the throng in the direction of the great auditorium. The men parted for them and turned to follow once they'd passed.

"Shall we gather at the river," Ira asked in song, "where bright angel feet have trod?"

A few voices joined him, but they were hesitant. Ira looked meaningfully at his friends, and they raised the song with him.

"With its crystal tide forever flowing by the throne of God."

The sound grew as they reached the familiar chorus.

"Yes, we'll gather at the river, the beautiful, the beautiful river; gather with the saints at the river that flows by the throne of God."

Ira sang the way into the Opera House, where even his great voice became lost in the shuffle of hundreds settling into their seats. People continued to flow in long after each chair was taken. They stood along the sides, in the aisles, and back to the door.

Moody waited until all was quiet, and then began as if he'd never left off.

"Is it too great a sacrifice, this life of a soldier for Christ? Matthew the gospel writer thought not. He recorded these words of Christ, which we find in chapter 11: 'Come unto me, all ye that labor and are heavy laden, and I will give you rest. Take my yoke upon you, and learn of me; for I am meek and lowly in heart: and ye shall find rest for your souls. For my yoke is easy and my burden is light.' Friends, what sacrifices would you not make for the One who can assure you a soul at rest?"

The silence in the hall was even more profound than that on the street corner, with all the outdoor noises of life shut out. Moody spoke until the convention delegates began to arrive for their evening session.

"Now we must close, as the brethren of the convention wish to come in to discuss the question 'How to reach the masses,' " he said, without a trace of irony. But Ira felt what Moody did not express. Here in this room, dozens would gather to talk in learned words of how to accomplish something that Moody had just managed with a simple message—and a song to draw his listeners.

Ira had no points to make, no strong arguments, when Moody once more raised the subject of their partnership. But he could not bring himself to make any commitment.

"I must speak to my wife," he said.

"I would expect nothing less," Moody said. "Please convey to her the need and the powerful work you have already seen God ready to do. The harvest is plentiful, Mr. Sankey, but He requires laborers to bring it in."

"I will speak to her," Ira repeated.

"And pray," Moody added.

Ira nodded. He couldn't meet Moody's eyes with their piercing urgency. Instead he shook the smaller man's hand briefly, settled his hat on his head, and stepped into the carriage waiting to take the Pennsylvania delegation to the train station.

Ira was in as much agony on the trip home as he had been in anticipation on the trip west.

He tried to sleep, but found his head filled with the sweat-streaked faces of men. He looked out the window, and they looked back, wondering why he would not want them to know what he knew.

He tried to distract himself in conversation with McMillan and the others. But they turned the talk to Moody in moments and he withdrew into his own thoughts again.

Ira turned thirty that August.

After dinner on his birthday, Fanny slipped out to the kitchen and returned carrying his favorite treat, a soft white cake with the boiled chocolate frosting she had perfected before they were married. She had made it often in those days, when Ira would come by her parents' house for dinner and sit a long while afterward in the parlor.

She placed the cake in front of him and smiled.

"Sweets for my sweet one."

Ira took the knife and carefully laid neat slices on plates for his parents, then cut two more for Fanny and himself.

Conversation swirled around him, but all he could hear was Moody's voice. A telegram in his pocket spoke to him as clearly as if the man stood before him.

"NEED YOU FIELDS ARE WHITE ARE YOU PRAYING"

It was unsigned but Ira knew why Moody hadn't bothered with the extra words. They weren't necessary.

The men had exchanged letters and telegrams regularly since their June meeting. Each conversation left Ira more agitated. He could not escape the need when Moody kept reminding him. But he could not see his way to part with all that was dear and familiar for some unproven, unfunded plan.

He didn't realize he'd laid down his fork until Fanny laid her hand on his sleeve.

"Ira?"

"I'm sorry, my dear. It's wonderful," he said, taking his first bite after he spoke.

"You've heard from Mr. Moody again," Fanny replied.

"Yes."

"Moody again?" said David Sankey. "Really, Ira, you must settle this thing. Are you joining the man or aren't you?"

Ira set his fork on his plate and was silent.

———————————

All fall the telegrams continued. Sometimes there were letters too, pleas that were urgent if not eloquent.

It wasn't that Ira didn't believe in Moody's cause. It wasn't even Moody himself; Ira respected the man and his methods.

It was home. It was Fanny and the boys and everything familiar. It was—he admitted in the darkest part of the night when Fanny breathed easily but he was not granted sleep—fear. Fear of the unknown. Fear of uncertain wages. Fear of unreceptive audiences. Fear of what might be and what might not.

Christmas fell on a Sunday that year. Ira and the choir had met for long hours preparing a special set of songs for the service.

On Christmas Eve when everyone else was sleeping, Ira sat up by the fire, organizing his sheaf of music. His eyes scanned the words to "God Rest Ye, Merry Gentlemen," as he slipped it into its place.

"Let nothing you dismay."

He read it once and then again.

"Let nothing you dismay, for Jesus Christ our Savior was born upon this day; to save us all from Satan's power when we were gone astray. O tidings of comfort and joy."

Ira was too practical to make much of the last verse. Still, he lingered over its opening phrase.

"Now to the Lord sing praises all you within this place."

6

"Scatter Seeds of Kindness"

A week. That's what Ira promised Moody—and God. He would give Chicago seven days and see what mark it left upon his heart.

Again Fanny tended to his clothes and brushed his hat. Ira bought a little book with empty pages and pasted in it some of his favorite texts and tunes. He wanted to have plenty of music ready at a moment's notice.

The train west was drafty, and Ira huddled into his overcoat, trying to find some pocket of warmth he had overlooked. He had no idea what was before him. Would they spend every day on crates, singing and preaching on street corners? Did Moody have large halls reserved each evening?

He really knew so little of the man, he realized. Yes, he'd read plenty about Moody's preaching with its stories to which everyone could relate and its piercing questions at the end. He knew of Moody's leadership in the YMCA and his flourishing Sunday school.

But what did the man do all day long? What would Ira do all day long?

He reached Chicago as the sun was rising. Moody had arranged a boarding house room for him for the week. Ira made his way there and gratefully accepted the breakfast that was just being served. After settling his things in his room, he walked to Moody's house on the side of the city.

Moody drew him in and straight to the parlor.

"Mr. Sankey! There you are. Will you please take a seat at the organ and lead us in some songs for our family time of devotion?"

They sang several songs; Moody read a passage of Scripture and prayed at length. All this concluded, Ira finally was introduced to the rest of the family—Moody's wife, Emma, and their daughter and two sons.

Ira had time for only the briefest of polite comments before Moody was at his elbow, steering him to the door.

"I'll be visiting many sick folk today, brothers and sisters as well as strangers to the Lord. I want you to sing for them," he said.

Ira obediently followed as Moody led out at a quick pace. Though Ira was the taller of the two, he seemed to require two strides to keep up with each of Moody's rapid ones.

"What would you like me to sing?" he asked to Moody's back.

"Oh, anything. You'll know what is right, I'm sure," Moody said without turning around.

His manner slowed noticeably when they entered the first house. Their object was a young mother, a woman whose large brood gathered from all corners when Moody stepped through the door.

The woman was half-sitting. She smiled at Moody and inclined her head to a chair placed near the head of her bed. He stepped softly to it and sat down on its very edge.

"I will read to you again today," he said. "But first, I have brought my friend Mr. Sankey, and he will sing for you."

Moody slid to the back of the chair, leaned against its slats, and gave his full attention to Ira, who stood like a tree at the foot of the bed, all angles and height and wildly out of place.

Ira waited only a half second before he began to sing.

"Let us gather up the sunbeams, lying all around our path; let us keep the wheat and roses, casting out the thorns and chaff; let us find our sweetest comfort in the blessings of today, with a patient hand removing all the briars from the way."

His voice filled the room, which was silent but for the crackling fire. Ira caught the eye of a boy who looked about ten and gave a small nod. Then there were two voices for the chorus.

"Then scatter seeds of kindness, then scatter seeds of kindness."

More joined in.

"Then scatter seeds of kindness for our reaping by and by."

Ira heard Moody's voice too, low but distinct among the children's more delicate tones. The other man was smiling as they finished.

"Fine. Thank you, Mr. Sankey. Shall we read Psalm 61 today, Ann? 'Hear my cry, O God; attend unto my prayer. From the end of the earth will I cry to thee, when my heart is overwhelmed.' "

The week was full of many such visits.

As they walked, Moody filled Ira's head with facts that supported his passion for this place. Chicago had been a lively, coltish town anyway, but with the growth of the railroads, it rapidly was becoming a teeming, wild city. At least fifteen rail lines stopped or originated in Chicago by the time Ira first visited.

"Nearly four hundred percent population growth in just a decade, Mr. Sankey. That's what they say anyway,"

Moody said. "And more coming every day. The world is a smaller place than it was when we were children."

Ira met the ailing and the widowed from Illinois Street Church, Moody's flock. They held meetings at the church too and at others in the city. At noon Ira sang and Moody spoke at prayer meetings in the business district.

Moody expressed repeated satisfaction with Ira's contributions. "Thank you, Mr. Sankey," he might say. Or, "That's just what was called for, Mr. Sankey." Or, "The Lord put that song in your heart tonight, Mr. Sankey."

On the last evening of Ira's visit, Moody was to lead a service at Farwell Hall, the meeting place of the Chicago YMCA. He pulled Ira aside before the sermon and requested a song.

" 'Come Home, O Prodigal Child,' which I heard you sing in Indianapolis," he said.

For most of the week, Moody had left the choice of songs to Ira. He had made no comments to indicate any displeasure at the selections, and Ira had even, by that last day, begun to feel a bit more comfortable with his own ideas.

But that night Moody would preach from Luke 15. The story of the prodigal son was one of his favorites, judging by the number of times he'd already addressed it. And he chose to leave no detail undone, right down to the song to tug softened hearts after he finished.

Ira had no objection. He knew the song and liked it.

But a deep hesitance, almost loathing, came over him when the time to sing drew near. The song was taking on personal implications that he wasn't prepared to entertain. Instead of calling Moody's wayward Christians back to the flock or drawing some sinner away from the brink of destruction, the song seemed to be written for him.

Come home. But where was home? Was it back in Lawrence County with Fanny and the boys? Or was it possible Chicago was now to be his home?

Ira finished the song, and the service was over. Instead of joining the men in the prayer room as he had done the rest of the week, he begged their understanding and explained he needed to pack for the trip home.

But back in his room, he left his trunk open at the foot of the bed and knelt by the window.

He looked out at the stars and smiled to think Fanny could see them too. But then he looked down into the street. Even at that late hour, he could see people. Most walked heading home, he supposed, from something. He saw the glowing lights of a tavern down the block and knew if he opened his window he'd hear laughter billowing up in the night air.

In the hall outside his room, a heavy footfall told him another visitor had bid Chicago goodnight and was coming in to sleep. What mark did the city leave on that man, Ira wondered? Would he leave it, whenever he left it, with a pang mixed with frustration that so foreign a place could cause a pang?

Ira thought he would sleep restlessly, but the week had worn on him more than he judged. He slept heavily and awoke only when sunlight slipped between the window frame and the edge of the drapery.

Moody was at the train station before Ira arrived. He was pacing in front of an empty bench.

"Sankey!" he said as Ira approached. "I have held my tongue for the week, but it is time to speak. Surely you see the good you have done, the help you have been in my meetings. It cannot have escaped you. The thing is settled in my mind: You should give up your work and come to Chicago at once."

Unlike at their first meeting in Indianapolis, Ira was at least prepared.

"Mr. Moody, it has been a tremendous privilege to serve with you," he said. "I have seen God at work in your ministry and have enjoyed being some small part of the effort. I assure you I will be in prayer about your offer and will give you my final word soon."

"I suppose I can ask for no more," Moody said. "Godspeed, Ira. I will pray for the train that brings you back."

———————————

Fanny could not get as much out of Ira as she wanted.

"And what did the sick ones say when you finished singing?" she asked. "Were they pleased? Did you let them choose songs or choose ones of your own liking?"

And another morning: "How many men did you say came to those evening meetings? Were some of them the same who'd been to the prayer meetings or were they all new faces?"

And another: "Where would you live if you went, Ira? Does Mr. Moody have a plan for you? I wonder if we should all go."

"Fanny, there's no need to talk of us all going, when it's not at all certain that I'll be going."

"Ira, you should talk to Robert," Fanny said. "I know he has been praying for you earnestly. He mentioned it several times that week you were gone. I think he could help you see this thing more clearly."

Ira sighed.

"Fanny, our own pastor thinks I should go. Why should I seek the opinion of another, even a good friend?"

"When did you speak to him?" Fanny asked, startled.

"This afternoon," Ira said. "I was going to tell you."

"Ira," she said. "Why are you fighting this? God has given you a gift. And now He has given you a very special way to use it."

"You sound like McMillan," Ira said.

"So you've asked his advice too?"

"I don't have to ask. It's in every conversation, every significant look when I try to explain why I might stay here."

"Then—"

"Fanny, I will do this. I see it is my duty, and I see how much you want it for me. But I cannot help being heavy-hearted at all I leave behind. I will not bring you and the boys to that rough place, so far from our families. I cannot ask you to join me in a venture that even I don't fully understand."

Fanny bit her lip and looked down for just a moment.

"Yes, I know, Ira," she said. "I've suspected for some time that this was the conclusion you must reach. We will wait for you and join you gladly the moment you call."

He pulled her close and laid his cheek on her head. She didn't feel the tears that ran into her hair.

7

"The Storm of Justice Falls, and Death is Nigh"

Once in Chicago Ira didn't have much time to ponder any regrets. Moody put him to work immediately and the two were constantly on the move. They made countless home visits, singing and praying with those who were ill. They led daily prayer meetings at noon and services again many evenings. Moody continued to preach at Illinois Street Church and was busy with the ever-growing Sunday school.

The new team ministered to some of its largest groups in Farwell Hall, the first home of the Chicago YMCA. The building on Madison Street, a few blocks from the courthouse, was dedicated in 1869. It was actually the second Farwell Hall—the first had burned less than a year after it was built.

Fires were commonplace in cities in the late 1800s. Most buildings were constructed entirely of wood. Those covered with stone or brick were still framed and floored with wood. Even some pillars and carvings that looked like stone or marble were actually painted wood. And in 1871, Chicago was crisscrossed by more than fifty-five miles of streets of pine. Its residents walked from place to place on more than six hundred miles of wooden sidewalks.

On a windy Sunday evening in October, Moody preached to a crowd that filled Farwell Hall all the way back to its doors. For five nights he had spoken about the life of Christ from His birth to His death and resurrection. It was after 9 p.m. when Moody began to close.

"Christ Himself made plain His purpose for coming. Listen again to the passage from John 3: 'And as Moses lifted up the serpent in the wilderness, even so must the Son of man be lifted up: That whosoever believeth in him should not perish, but have eternal life.'

"This week we have seen the baby Christ, we have observed Him as a man, suffering a brutal death, and we have discovered Him to be victorious over even that death. And now I want you to ask yourselves, 'What should I do with Jesus?' " Moody said. "Will you consider that question this week? Will you consider His work and the need of your soul? And will you come back next week and tell me what you have concluded? Mr. Sankey, sing for us, please."

Ira rose beside the organ at the back of the platform. The organist played a chord, and Ira began to sing.

"Today the Savior calls: ye wand'rers, come; o ye benighted souls, why longer roam?"

As he sang, bells could be heard outside. A few heads turned, a few people stirred, but most stayed focused on Ira and the song.

"Today the Savior calls: o listen now! Within these sacred walls to Jesus bow."

The summer had been viciously dry. Now, in the fall, five or six fires would break out around the city each day. With them came the bells of the fire engines and sometimes the great bell in the cupola of the courthouse, sounding a general alarm.

"Today the Savior calls: for refuge fly; the storm of justice falls, and death is nigh."

Just that morning the *Chicago Tribune* had urged residents not to grow so accustomed to the bells that they became just another harmony in the city's background noises.

"For days past alarm has followed alarm, but the comparatively trifling losses have familiarized us to the pealing of the Courthouse bell, and we [have] forgotten that the absence of rain for three weeks [has] left everything in so dry and inflammable a condition that a spark might set a fire which would sweep from end to end of the city," the paper warned.

Ira had read the editorial while he finished his coffee and struggled to remember if he'd heard bells the day before or not.

"We are certainly growing dull to the alarm," he said aloud to the paper. He spoke to it often, a poor substitution for his usual talks with Fanny and the boys over the day's news.

That night by the time Ira finished the third verse, the noises outside were impossible to ignore any longer. The endless bells were starting to bother the crowd. People fidgeted and looked anxious.

Moody brought the meeting to an abrupt close. Thousands of people streamed out of Farwell Hall and into the streets.

Near the fire, there was confusion and fear. But just blocks away, as other Sunday services dismissed, people strolled and visited, paying no attention to the smoke. Only the night before, a fire barely a half mile from Farwell Hall had burned four blocks of the city. It took most of the day to get that one under control.

On October 8, people expected the same thing—another fire that would be handled in its time.

Moody and Ira took a back way out of the building and had their first glimpse of the flames. The fire was just a light in the distance then, a glow perhaps ten blocks away on the city's west side.

The bells grew more demanding as the wind whipped and swirled from the southwest, sailing the flames forward into the heart of the city. Moody should go home to his family, they decided. Ira planned to go toward the fire and try to help.

They shook hands.

"Take care, Ira," Moody said.

"And you do the same, Mr. Moody."

Shoving his hat firmly onto his head, Ira bent into the gale and headed for the river. In the tunnels formed between the taller buildings, the wind was a solid force pushing against him.

He crossed the bridge on Madison Street, and then turned south. The flames were like a lighthouse, revealing the location of their own danger.

An entire block of small buildings was engulfed. Ira joined a band of men who were pulling down board fences. They raced to take away the fuel the fire would need to spread farther.

But the heat and the wind were at work far above the men's heads, carrying burning bits of homes, furniture, and clothing to rooftops blocks away.

"Help me here!" one man shouted at Ira.

"It's no use," another said. "We can't stop it. Save yourself."

The second man ran, but the first cried again, "Help me!"

Ira rushed to his side and pulled with him at the pine fence. A chunk of ash landed on his neck. He jumped and brushed it away before it could singe his skin. The other man's leather hat was rippling from the heat.

Ira grabbed the man at the wrist and pulled him back from the fence.

"We must leave here," he said.

The man shook his wrist free and glared into Ira's eyes.

"My house is there," he growled, pointing up the block, "beside the tracks."

"Please go then, and get what you can and leave," Ira said. "This city is doomed."

He clapped the man's shoulder for a moment, and then ran back toward the bridge. Farwell Hall was less than ten blocks away. The fire would be there before long.

Firefighters, too, were losing the battle. Hoses burst. Embers carried in the sky for blocks fell to ignite new fires all around. More burning debris fell on Ira too, as he hurried back to the hall. He shook the bits from his coat and hair and kept moving.

Inside the building, he rushed to the small room that had been serving as his apartment. Ira threw things hastily into bags and a trunk and stacked them by the door. Then he ran back outside to look for a cart or wagon.

It was after midnight, but beside the raging fire the streets had been as light as day. While it was darker here, Ira knew the fierce light was coming his way.

He heard the clattering of hooves before he saw the horse. It was racing up Clark Street, pulling a wagon that rattled and rocked. A small crowd of men ran behind the animal, trying to grab the wagon or the reins. Ira rushed forward, but before the horse reached him, it turned a corner and fell in its haste. The men climbed around and on top of it, heedless of the animal's pain. There was shouting and shoving. Ira backed away quickly. He wanted no part of that quarrel.

With no wagon and no beast to do the job, he'd have to do it himself.

He stuffed what he could into two large valises and headed east toward Lake Michigan. As he passed a construction site near the intersection of State and Monroe, an idea struck him: Palmer House, an elegant hotel, was built just to street level. Its massive foundation surrounded underground rooms and passages. Ira thought his things would be safe there, at least for a time. He used a wooden plank to ease himself into the cellar, found a dark corner, and stowed his bags.

He climbed out and returned to Farwell Hall for more of his belongings. When he saw folks leaning out of their windows, craning for a view, he called to them.

"You must leave. It's not safe. The fire will be here soon."

"Have you seen it? How close is it?" one woman asked.

"It began across the river, but it's already crossed over," Ira said. "The wind, it's blowing it toward us. These blocks will burn. Please, leave now."

She pulled her head in, not taking time even to thank him.

Ira began to carry a second load toward the lake. The streets already were brighter than they had been a few minutes before. The air was filled with burning bits that were almost beautiful. They reminded Ira of thick, swirling snowflakes during a spring storm. But instead of shimmering silver, these flakes were sparkling gold.

He left his things on the stone steps of a large house and returned to Farwell Hall for the last time. Loaded down, he retraced his steps to the house, planning to combine his things and carry as much as he could to the lakefront.

But people were beginning to pour out of all the homes in that section of town. Many had the same ideas as Ira. When he found the house where he'd left his things, he was dismayed to see the steps had disappeared under a pile of boxes and bags several feet deep.

He labored a short distance, and then found two men with an empty stretcher who were willing to help him. But before they reached the lake, they saw the fire moving southward, toward their homes. They did not ask for the pay Ira had promised; they simply dropped the stretcher in the middle of the street and ran.

Ira finally reached the lake. He pushed his trunk as close to the water as he dared. If the fire came all the way to the edge, he planned to swim out and save himself from the heat.

Ira sat down on the trunk to catch his breath, and then remembered his bags in the Palmer House. He hauled himself up once more and walked quickly back to the streets. The bags were where he had left them.

After settling his belongings into a small pile, Ira asked a man nearby—on his own small pile—to keep an eye on the baggage while he went to get a drink. He was parched from the heat and the work of the last few hours.

He knocked at an elegant house on Wabash Avenue and asked for water. A maid directed him to a faucet in the rear of the building. Ira rushed to it, swallowing in anticipation, but air, not water, came out. The city's waterworks had burned down around 3 a.m. and its pumping machines were no longer moving any water.

Ira went back to the lake once more. He found his pile and fell down beside it. Trying to ignore his thirst, the light, and the noise, he shook his overcoat out like a blanket and dropped into a brief, exhausted sleep.

8

"By Faith We Can See It Afar"

After a surreal day in a boat on Lake Michigan, watching Chicago burn, Ira now was safe, if not clean, and on his way back to his family. At the first station away from the city, he left his rail car and hurried to the telegraph office. He knew news of the fire must have reached Fanny by now, and he was anxious to calm her fears.

"Safe," he wrote on the paper he would slide across the counter to the operator. "Returning home. Ira."

Returning home. What a strange feeling those words gave him. Just months ago he was loath to leave Pennsylvania. And now he reluctantly traveled back. It would be wonderful to see Fanny and the boys again. Surely he was not sorry to be heading toward them.

"But I will miss Chicago," he murmured to his reflection in the window. "I will miss it."

Stumpy fields that recently had been stripped of their crops began to slide by faster and faster as the train picked up speed heading east. Ira tried to focus on an individual broken stalk, but it disappeared as quickly as the thoughts slipping through his mind.

Fanny thought the countryside after harvest was barren and sad. She was always eager for the blanket of snow that would hide all traces of the snapped corn stalks. But Ira found them almost painfully beautiful. Everything they had of value they had given, and there they stood, motley, uneven, their gold fading to a dry yellow. And then, in spring, they would have one last gift to give, when they were plowed back into the fields where they started. To him, these fields cried out the promise of the future.

"There's a land that is fairer than day, and by faith we can see it afar; for the Father waits over the way to prepare us a dwelling place there."

He sang it in his head, not out loud. Then he stopped and sighed.

Chicago had been so much more than he expected. He cringed to remember how reluctantly he'd traveled the other direction on this same route in the spring.

Ira had worried at first that he wouldn't have enough to keep himself occupied. It took less than a week to realize the foolishness of that notion. Moody seemed tireless and filled his calendar accordingly; Ira went along to each appointment.

Shepherding the sick and needy of Moody's church alone was a full-time job. Moody wanted no one left unvisited, no care-worn soul passed over in prayer. Ira could see at first that it was Moody they wanted. It was he who made their eyes light with hope. But the songs were not unwelcome, and before long they were asking for more, asking for another after Moody had read a Psalm and prayed.

The noon prayer meetings were beyond Ira's imagination. Men, and some women, came from across the city to meet for that hour. Their hearts were burdened, their prayers impassioned. There was little music at these meetings as time was short, but Ira wasn't sorry. He loved listening to the prayers rising up around the room.

He and Moody hadn't taken long to understand each other in the evening meetings. At the start, Moody might suggest a song that matched his text or perhaps something

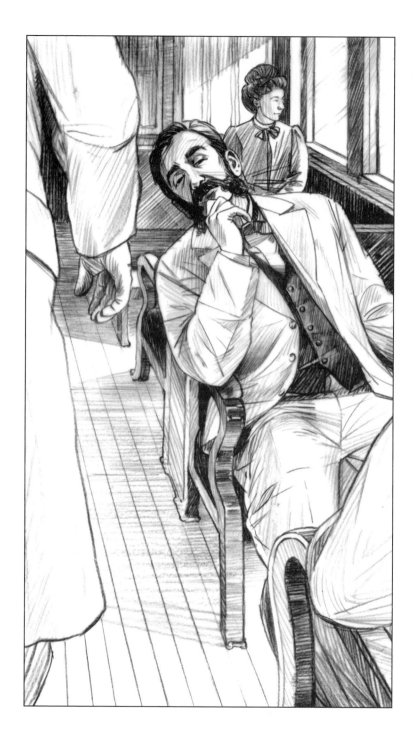

poignant to soften hardened hearts when it was time to invite men and women to the inquiry room.

But soon Moody left the music entirely to Ira. He planned the songs the congregation would sing, selected solos to use before Moody preached, and chose pieces to make a final plea for repentance after Moody so powerfully laid the groundwork of the gospel.

Ira realized he must have dozed off when he heard the conductor call the New Castle station. He pressed his fingers to the corners of his eyes and stifled a yawn. He supposed he would have to reapply for his job with the revenue department. But surely they had filled the position by now. It was more than six months since he'd left.

He sighed again, shrugged into his smoky-smelling overcoat, and adjusted his sleeves. He'd deal with that tomorrow. For now he wanted nothing more than Fanny and his boys, a bath, and his bed, with perhaps a small dinner somewhere in between.

Ira's rest lasted two months. His old position had been filled, as he expected, but he was placed in a new job in the same office. Chicago began to take on a dreamlike quality.

Ira read the papers as voraciously as ever and knew Chicago was being rebuilt at break-neck speed. He scanned daily for word of Moody or the YMCA or the Illinois Street Church. The latter was over the river, eight blocks north of Farwell Hall, but Ira had seen drawings and maps showing the extent of the fire. He knew it had burned well beyond where he'd been that dreadful night.

"Well," he said one morning, "I see here the new courthouse will use the same bell as the old."

"What courthouse?" Fanny said.

"Oh, Chicago, dear," Ira said, bending his paper forward to show her the front page of the *Tribune*. He'd been having papers mailed to him since he arrived back in Pennsylvania.

"Are they making much progress?" Fanny said, pouring more coffee into Ira's cup.

"Seem to be," he said. "Every day there's more about this building or that reopening."

"And anything of Moody?"

"No, nothing. Not yet."

She looked at him for a long moment, but said no more.

When a telegraph from Chicago arrived that afternoon, Fanny bundled Harry and Eddie into their coats and hurried them to her mother's house. She rushed to Ira's office and laid the slip on his desk almost triumphantly.

"It must be Moody," she said.

"Did you read it?"

"Of course not. Hurry!"

Ira unfolded the page and scanned its contents in seconds.

"Well?"

"He's rebuilding," Ira said. "He asks me to return. The work in Chicago will go forward."

"Oh, Ira!" Fanny couldn't contain her smile.

"I am glad," he said. "I do not deny it. But Fanny, I cannot leave you again."

"We'll go with you, Ira. We can go. I want to go."

"I want you to as well. But I'll go first and see how the city fares, find a place where you and the boys will be safe and comfortable. I think we can stand another separation if we know it has an end."

She walked around the desk and held out her hands. Ira took them and squeezed them gently.

"God is good to us, Ira."

"He is, Fanny. He is."

9

"Let Me Hide Myself in Thee"

Ira had been wise to leave Fanny and the boys in Pennsylvania. The Chicago he returned to remained a skeleton of the city he'd left, at least at its heart. But he walked the streets with a smile on his face, glad to find he still recognized major intersections, still remembered his way from one place to another.

There were new buildings everywhere he looked. And among them were hulking remnants the fire had gutted, the places that remained to be rebuilt and refurbished.

Moody's church on Illinois Street did not live to see a new beginning. But a new, temporary building that everyone was calling the Tabernacle was already housing Sunday services and prayer meetings.

Ira moved into the Tabernacle with Moody. The preacher had lost his home and most of his belongings. Moody enjoyed telling the story of his wife urging him to carry an oil painting of himself as they fled before the fire.

"My dear," he would repeat to whoever listened, "think of what people would say of a man who would save naught but his own portrait on a night like this one."

He always finished with the same line: "All I saved was my Bible, my family, and my reputation."

Ira now joined Moody in a new work: Raising funds to rebuild his church and to help those who were left with nothing after the fire. Ira was in awe of Moody's boldness and skill with people regarding such a delicate matter.

Moody stopped him once as they were on their way to visit a church member.

"A moment, please, Sankey. I know that fellow across the street."

Without waiting to see if Ira would follow, Moody glanced both ways then hurried over to a tall man in a dark coat.

"Martin!" he said. "I am so glad to see you today. You are just the fellow I needed to run across. I'd like you to give one thousand dollars to help rebuild the Illinois Street church."

Ira reached their sides in time to hear the last sentence, and he could not hide his shock.

Mr. Martin was at least as surprised.

"I'm sorry, I can't help you, Moody," he said. "I haven't got it."

"You could borrow it though," Moody said.

Ira watched Martin's face soften from displeasure to amusement.

"Never without an answer, are you?" he said. "Borrow it. So I could. And so I shall. You will have your check tomorrow."

Nothing could surprise Ira after that, he decided. And so he was not at all shocked the next day when the check arrived, along with another, larger one, from a colleague Martin had spoken to shortly after encountering Moody on the street.

The noon prayer meetings seemed even more crowded than in the days before the fire. Ira supposed there were more people in town, drawn by the jobs that came with rebuilding. Moody prayed the attendance was a sign of a spiritual awakening in people who had seen their liveli-hoods—and even their lives—in mortal danger.

The days were packed for Moody, and Ira was always at his side. They visited the sick most mornings. At noon they assembled for prayer meeting. While the meeting it-self was only an hour, Moody and Ira were there until at least 2, speaking quietly or praying with those who stayed behind, sometimes in tears.

Many nights Moody gave a Bible lecture in one of the churches or some public building. These meetings often drew more than a thousand. Moody's talks were thick with Scripture and, in these cases, short on stories. He read passage after passage, commenting on each as he wove them together into a compact doctrinal lesson.

The evangelistic meetings typically began at 7 and they often were followed by a meeting especially for young men around 9 or 9:30.

Many wondered at the results God gave to Moody and Ira. They might well have wondered at the physi-cal strength and energy He gave as well. These were not schedules for the faint of heart.

Sundays, too, were full. A first service was held at City Hall at 9, another at Moody's church at 11, and two more in the evening, the first for women and the second for men.

When Moody asked Ira to take a class in the Chicago Sunday school, Ira didn't hesitate.

His lessons were soon in great demand, in part because he was one of few teachers who started class with songs. Ira was a strict instructor though. He expected quiet at-tention when the lecture began and dismissed students who were the least bit unruly.

In his classes, young men from all walks of Chicago life learned about the Bible's message to them. Ira was as insistent on clarity in his classroom instruction as he was on clarity in his diction as he sang.

By the fall of 1872, Chicago had begun to resemble its former self. Ira decided it was time to bring Fanny, Harry, and Eddie to the city.

Fanny was overjoyed to be reunited with her husband and eager to know his partner about whom she'd heard so much. But she had to wait a bit longer for the latter meeting.

Just before the rest of the Sankey family arrived in Chicago, Moody left for his second evangelistic trip to England. While he was away, Ira and several other men shared the responsibilities at the Tabernacle, in Sunday school, and with the many spiritually and physically needy souls who looked to Moody for leadership and help.

Chicago was a wild city to Fanny, who was accustomed to the quieter, more refined nature of New Castle. But she grew to love the work, as Ira had, and soon was hurrying around town, Harry at her side and Eddie on her hip, to meet Ira at one home or another or to sit with a widow or bring a meal to an invalid.

She was with him the day he was called to visit a dying child.

Fanny tried to hide her revulsion at the miserable conditions in the small home. Not one surface was properly clean. Even the children seemed layered in old dirt.

The sick one was a bit cleaner than the rest, a result of his mother wiping his fevered forehead over and over with a damp rag.

"Child," Ira said, "I am told you know your days here are short."

"Yes," the boy said.

"Are you a Christian, son? Do you know our Savior, Jesus?"

"Yes, sir."

"I am glad to hear it. When did you come to know Him?"

The boy made a visible effort to gather his strength for the answer.

"Do you remember last Thursday in the Tabernacle, when we had that little singing meeting and you sang, 'Jesus Loves Even Me'?"

"Yes, yes, I remember," Ira said. "You were there?"

"I was there. It was the last time I left the house. Last Thursday. I believed on the Lord Jesus that day, and now I am going to be with Him this day."

Fanny had been standing against the wall behind Ira. But now she moved past him to sit on the edge of the bed. She met eyes with the grieving mother and gently took the rag from her hands.

"Rest, child. And rest, madam. Let me soothe him for a few minutes while you just lay with him."

When Moody returned, he found that the Mr. Sankey he had left behind was now part of a splendid team. With Fanny at his side, Ira was effective in new ways and even more enthusiastic about the truth.

Moody scarcely had time to catch his breath before they boarded a train for Springfield where they'd been invited to hold special services.

Ira enjoyed Fanny's amazement as she first saw the evangelist at work. The committee that had invited them had made arrangements for a hall and prepared handbills to advertise the meetings. But Moody saw no need to wait for the appointed time.

"Come, Sankey," he said once they'd settled their luggage in their rooms. "I saw a likely corner as we came from the station."

Ira found his own crate now, or sometimes a cart or wagon that was available. He sang without being asked.

"There is a fountain filled with blood drawn from Immanuel's veins; and sinners plunged beneath that flood lose all their guilty stains."

Fanny stood to one side and watched a crowd gather, slowly at first, then rapidly, as people hurried to see what they were missing. Some joined Ira at the chorus.

"Lose all their guilty stains, lose all their guilty stains; and sinners plunged beneath that flood lose all their guilty stains."

Ira stepped down, and Moody was already up in his place.

"Brothers, that fountain flowed for you," he said. "Immanuel's veins were drawn for you. You, sir, are the ruined, helpless sinner, but you can plunge in and find your sin stains gone forever, as so many already have. We are going now to speak more of these matters. Will you join us, friends?"

Ira was singing again. Fanny hadn't even heard his first words, she was so focused on Moody and watching the crowd respond to him.

"Let me hide myself in Thee," he sang.

Rock of Ages. Cleft for me. The blood from Immanuel's veins, spilled for guilty sinners. Fanny felt tears pooling and blinked them away. Ira was singing God's message to these people. And they were listening.

She clutched the boys closer and hurried after the surging crowd.

Philip Phillips, six years Ira's senior, had been teaching others to sing since he was a teen. Like Ira's only teacher, William Bradbury, Phillips led singing schools across many states. He eventually began a solo career in which he presented services of sacred music.

Phillips had just completed a tour of Europe where he had sung for one hundred consecutive nights. He was ready now to tour the Pacific coast of the United States. And he wanted Ira to join him.

Ira fiddled with the delicate handle of his coffee cup. When he'd received Phillips's telegram saying he'd arrive that evening, Fanny had rushed to lay out the best things for their evening meal. Their small apartment was dark, but she made the most of every ray of natural light and warmed the whole space with bright curtains and plenty of lamps.

"Ira, this job is clearly suited to your skills and your interests," Phillips said. "I wish you could have seen the crowds in England, pressing in close so no one missed a word. They were hanging on the gospel, Ira. I tell you, I've never seen anything like it here. There is truly some spiritual awakening going on there."

Ira thought of the Chicago street corners and the crowd in Springfield. He opened his mouth to offer a counterpoint, but Phillips was speaking again.

"I believe God can do the same work in this country," he said, and Ira nodded.

"I've seen it, Philip," he said. "I've seen it right here in Chicago."

"Yes, of course, I know Moody's work is magnificent. I don't mean to suggest otherwise. I'm only saying, Ira, think what we could do together. Think of the services we could hold with two voices, giving each other rests as needed. We could go for two hundred nights, I'm sure of it, traveling all up and down the coast."

Ira nodded, but he was thinking, not agreeing. Phillips misunderstood.

"It will be a blessing to serve with you, sir," he said. "And you need not have a minute's worry about financial matters. My sponsors will cover all your expenses, and they offer a generous salary besides."

"Philip, I cannot make a commitment tonight," Ira said.

"Right, of course. Think it over. Talk to Fanny," Phillips said, nodding in her direction.

"To Fanny, yes, and I must speak to Moody as well."

Phillips grasped Ira's hand tightly as he left.

"Ira, the Lord can use you in this ministry. I know it."

"I am grateful for your confidence, and I will not leave you waiting long for your answer."

Ira closed the door behind Phillips and turned to face Fanny.

"You said very little, my dear," he said.

"I was trying to read your heart, Ira."

She passed him his hat—he hadn't even noticed it in her hand. She had gone for it while he was seeing Phillips out.

"Go speak to Mr. Moody. Pray with him. God will direct you, Ira. I know He will."

Ira took his hat but instead of putting it on, he stood looking at her.

"I don't deserve a wife as wise and good as you, Fanny."

She laughed.

"Go."

A warm lamp glow washed out of many windows onto the darkening street as Ira headed for Moody's house. As he knocked on the door, he realized too late that Moody might be at supper with his family.

"Ira! Come in, come in," Moody said, drawing him into the light of the front hall. "Is everything well with you?"

The Sankeys and Moodys were in each other's homes often but a drop-in visit was unusual.

"Oh, we're well, Mr. Moody," said Ira, who still couldn't bring himself to call Moody "Dwight." "I wondered if you might have a few moments for a conversation and prayer."

"Of course, Ira, of course. Here, sit down, please."

Ira settled into a chair and Moody took the seat opposite. Ira spun his hat round and round in his hands, and then finally spoke.

"Philip Phillips has asked me to join him on a singing tour of the west," he said. "He had a tremendous reception in Europe and expects no less in California. He is confident that together we could minister to even more souls and spread the gospel wider still than he could alone. He asks me to leave with him within the month."

Moody listened with no change in his expression. He only leaned forward into his chair to look full in Ira's face.

"And what is it you would like us to pray about?" he said.

"I don't know whether I should go," Ira said. "He makes a compelling case but I am just not sure."

"Then we will ask our Lord to make you sure, to show you His path, and to give you His confidence."

The lamps in the sitting room burned well into the night. Ira listened to his friend pour out his heart and calm came to his own heart. He knew what he should do—what he would do.

10
"Do Not Pass Me By"

In early summer 1873, Philip Phillips took a train west, and Ira and Fanny sailed for England with Moody and his family.

Phillips had accepted Ira's decision graciously. "We would have been quite a team, Ira," he said. "But you are part of quite a team already. I know that. I wish you well. Write and tell me how you find England."

When Ira had informed Moody that he saw his way clearly, Moody had smiled broadly.

"I'm glad of it, my friend," he said. "Now I am free to propose another trip to you."

Moody had received an invitation from the Rev. William Pennefather and Cuthbert Bainbridge to hold services in England again. Word of Ira's work with Moody had reached the Continent, and they were inviting him too. Could they be in London by June, Pennefather wondered.

Moody had already accepted for himself. But he was eager for Ira to join him.

Ira took the invitation to Fanny, who shook her head and smiled.

"Ira Sankey, what will the Lord have for you next?" she said.

"So you think I should go?"

"Go? Of course you should go. Didn't you just say no to Mr. Phillips so you could keep working with Mr. Moody?"

"Well, I thought I was saying no to Phillips so I could work here in Chicago with Moody, Fanny. Surely you know that."

"Ira, you and Mr. Moody are a team. He needs you. These people are asking for you. The work is there to be done as well as here. If Mr. Moody can leave his pulpit and his flock in capable hands, why can't you do the same?"

"You make it sound so simple."

"Is it difficult?" she said. "Ira, look back. Look into your memory back to Indianapolis. Remember what you told me when Moody first asked you to join him? 'He's a powerful speaker,' you said, 'if a bit unrealistic in his plans for other men's lives.' And now you would resist and stay here in Chicago—a work you first rejected though he recommended it."

Ira could not meet her eyes. He stared into the flickering lamplight.

"Ira, remember after the fire? Remember your despair that you might never be useful again, that those few months were all that had been meant for you? Look back and then look forward, Ira. Look at what may be."

"I wish I could see things with your clarity and confidence, Fanny," Ira said. "I am sure you're right. But we will pray on it a day or two. I already told Moody as much."

"I would expect no less," she said.

"And where do you see yourself in these long views you take?" Ira said, a smile in his voice.

"In England," Fanny answered immediately. "In England with you."

And now here they were, aboard this great ship, en route to Europe. Until the last moment the trip had seemed little more than a dream. They had chosen a day to leave Chicago and had made arrangements accordingly, but there was not money enough to pay their passage.

Hours before their train was to leave Chicago, a friend who knew only that a trip was planned stopped by to wish them well. And he pressed Moody to accept five hundred dollars.

"A little something to help when you arrive, as you get settled," he said.

Moody seemed not a bit surprised, but he did laugh.

"It will not help *when* we arrive. It will allow us *to arrive*," he said.

Ira and Fanny had parted with difficulty from Harry and Eddie, who were staying with their grandparents. With so much uncertainty in their travel plans and accommodations, not to mention the anticipated hours of work each day, the boys were better off settled quietly in Pennsylvania.

But knowing the arrangement was practical did not make it any less emotional. Fanny held each boy tightly. Harry stood stiffly and accepted her embrace, his face somber. But when she dropped to her knees, Eddie wrapped his wiry arms around her neck, and then wound his legs around her waist and hung on her.

"Will you be home when I'm five, Mama?"

"Oh, Eddie, I don't know. But you will have Harry and Grandmother and Grandfather and a wonderful cake too, I'm sure."

"When I'm six?" he asked into her shoulder.

Fanny sighed deeply, almost a moan, and looked up at Ira.

"Son, God only knows," he said. "But we can trust His plan for you, just as we trust His plan for us."

Later, her tears over for the time, Fanny set about exploring the ship. This would be the great adventure of their lives, she said. Ira hoped it would meet her expectations.

The new voyagers fared better than their companions. Moody was in his room, ill, almost before land was out of sight. But Fanny and Ira took easily to life at sea and spent much of their time on deck, enjoying the wind and the vast view of water in every direction.

In the evenings Fanny sewed or read aloud, and Ira worked on something he was beginning to call his musical scrapbook.

While he carried many hymns in his head wherever he went, he had spent only a few weeks with Moody before he realized he needed a much deeper well from which to draw. He began collecting new hymns from many sources. Sometimes he would simply jot down the text of a poem he found moving. He'd read the words over and over, trying their meter with various familiar hymn tunes.

The book was little more than a bulging sheaf when they left port. By the time they landed in England, Ira had it organized neatly by topic. He had entertained Fanny by trying to set a few of the pieces to tunes of his own and had filed rough copies of those in the book as well.

Ira and Fanny were packed well before it was time for the passengers to disembark. They met Moody, still notably pale, on the way from their cabin.

"I was looking for you," he said. "We must pray before we go ashore."

"Certainly," Ira said. "Shall we find somewhere quiet?"

...

"Here," Moody said, waving his hand at an empty dining room. "This will do."

While they were still being seated, he laid a letter in front of Ira. But he summarized before Ira could read it.

"Pennefather and Bainbridge have both died, Sankey. They were to lead the meetings; they were the organizers, our hosts. It seems to me the Lord is closing this door. I don't know why He waited to give us this news until we were already here, but we shall simply follow as He leads. If we do not have some clear opening, we will return to America at once."

Fanny took Ira's hand, and he gripped hers tightly.

"So we are strangers in a strange land. No one has invited us, no one has made plans for us, and no one intends to pay us. Do I understand you?"

Fanny shot him a worried look but was quickly relieved. Ira was smiling.

"You do take this acting on faith rather seriously, don't you, Moody?"

Fanny smiled too.

"We're not worried, Mr. Moody," she said. "We shall enjoy England for now and wait with you to see whether we stay or go."

Now Moody smiled too.

"Well then," he said. "Good. I confess I was concerned you might not take this news so well. We shall see what is next. This letter was in a bundle I received just before we left the States. I have not finished reading through all the others. Who knows what they may contain?"

Finding solid ground a shock after so many days of using their sea legs, they hurried to settle themselves into a Liverpool hotel—and bed. Ira and Fanny talked long into the night.

"I don't know why I'm so sure, but I just know we're staying," Ira said. "I cannot believe God would bring us so far only to send us home. The waste of time and expense alone seems to argue against it, besides which we know there is a need here."

"I'm glad to hear you so sure, Ira," Fanny said.

"You have your own example to thank, my dear."

He pulled the quilt tighter around him and settled one last time into his pillow.

"I believe God may use this strange circumstance to show us that nothing that happens here in England will be of our doing. Our plans must fall apart so His can be accomplished."

"Well said, Ira. Now please, go to sleep."

Ira's theory began to prove true almost immediately.

Moody spent their first morning in England going through the rest of the correspondence he'd carried with him from Chicago. In his sickness he'd been unable to read or answer most of it while they were at sea.

Among the letters was one from the secretary of the York YMCA asking, "Should you ever travel to the country again, we would be so pleased to have you speak to our association. Please let us know if such an opportunity arises."

"This may be our new door, Sankey," Moody said. "It is already partly open. We will go there and begin our work."

The team split briefly while Moody settled his family in London, and Ira and Fanny traveled to Manchester to visit a cousin. When they arrived in York, Moody was already there.

No one had imagined they would arrive so soon—the letter requesting a visit had been sent only a few weeks ago—and the York leaders were urging a delay. So many families were away for annual trips to the sea. It was not a good time.

Ira listened to the conversation quietly. His partner seemed neither disappointed nor concerned.

"Can you rent a hall?" Moody asked. "That's all we shall need."

Notices were posted: Evangelistic Services. D. L. Moody of Chicago will preach and Ira D. Sankey of Chicago will sing at 7 o'clock p.m. tomorrow, Thursday, and each succeeding evening for a week, in the Independent Chapel. All are welcome. No collection.

Thursday night, Ira stood to sing and felt a twinge of dismay. Fewer than fifty people were in the room. He had been sitting in the front row, facing forward, as they arrived, and the bustle had made them sound like many more than they were.

He invited them to join him, but the songs were mostly solos that night. The visitors were clustered near the back of the room, as far from Ira and the pulpit as possible. Their expressions were uncertain as he sang.

"Pass me not, O gentle Savior, hear my humble cry; while on others Thou art calling, do not pass me by."

"Do you not know these songs?" he asked when he had finished "Pass Me Not." It had been written nearly five years before by Fanny Crosby and set to music by Howard Doane.

A few brave ones shook their heads.

"Ah, then I will teach them to you," Ira said.

He sang again the three pieces he had just sung. He thought he was imagining the few voices joining him on a chorus, but, no, there were some lips moving way in the back.

Moody jumped up to speak with the same energy Ira had witnessed a thousand times. He gave a short, urgent plea for their hearts to be soft, announced the daily noon prayer meetings and Bible studies to follow, and sat down again.

The crowd was a bit quieter as it left—more like the few dozen people it was than the many it had sounded coming in, Ira thought.

He sat next to Moody, who was praying silently.

Moody looked up, glanced around the empty room, and spoke.

"Sankey, I see a tiny cloud of blessing rising. It is no larger than a man's hand now, but I believe it will soon engulf us in showers and flood this dry ground."

11
"Free From the Law,
O Happy Condition"

No flood came to the first prayer meeting though.

Six people were all, two of them the York YMCA president and secretary. With Ira, Fanny, and Moody included there were nine.

Moody began each noon meeting by reading prayer requests that others had handed to him. Then he opened the floor to anyone who wanted to testify of God's work in his life. The rest of the hour was spent in prayer, the people divided into small groups.

The crowds grew steadily during that first week. But it was a silent, watchful lot that came. One occasionally would stand to offer a remark on the previous night's sermon, but there was none of the passion Ira had learned to expect at the Chicago prayer meetings.

Over breakfast, he pressed Moody for his thoughts.

"Should we consider another city, do you think?"

"This is the door God opened, Ira. It does not seem to me that He has completed His work here."

"But perhaps He has chosen another place to pour down His blessings of revival," Ira said, buttering his toast and not looking at Moody.

"I know you must be discouraged, Ira," Moody said.

"Aren't you?" Ira asked.

"Free From the Law, O Happy Condition"

"No. No, I am not. I believe these floodgates are going to open and we must be at the ready to draw in souls when they do."

Ira was thinking about his response when Moody spoke again.

"He began the good work, Ira. We had nowhere to go, and He sent us here. He will be faithful to complete this work, I think, and I believe you and I both recognize it is not completed now."

A week later, Moody opened another noon prayer meeting with the usual offer to speak of God's working in their lives. To Ira's surprise, a man stood.

"For two days I have been away from the meetings, closeted with my Master," he said.

Ira was sitting far to the front but was enough to one side to turn his neck hard and see the man's face. It was the Rev. F. B. Meyer, the young pastor of a large Baptist congregation in York.

"I think He has had the victory over my arrogance and pride," Meyer said. "And I believe I have made a full surrender of all to Him."

The room was quiet, but not the usual stoic absence of sound. It was a hushed, anticipating quiet.

Meyer had stopped and was swallowing hard. Finally, he spoke again.

"Will you pray for me, friends? I dearly long for the Spirit's blessing on every word that comes from my mouth."

Ira may have imagined it, but the murmured prayers that afternoon seemed energized by a greater intensity than he had yet seen in England. Meyer's humble admission and obvious joy at his renewed relationship with Christ seemed to stir hearts in a way that the preaching and songs had not yet done.

That one public submission to repentance soon turned into the flood Moody had been expecting. Hearts softened and word spread. Shortly the noon meetings were filled to capacity. People were turned away every evening and more workers were needed each night to meet people in the inquiry rooms.

Moody rejoiced in the crowds coming to hear of the Savior. But he never stopped calling for more to come, knowing that scores remained in ignorance about the state of their own souls.

One night he closed his message with an American Civil War story about a fort in the Kennesaw Mountains that was all but lost. General Sherman heard the men planned to surrender and sent back an urgent message: Hold.

"Our friend, Mr. Bliss, has written a hymn entitled 'Hold the Fort, for I am Coming,' and I'm going to ask Mr. Sankey to sing that hymn," Moody said. "I hope there will be thousands of young converts coming into the ranks to help hold the fort. Our Savior is in command, and He is coming."

As Ira sang, there was movement across the great room. People rose and walked with bowed heads to inquiry rooms.

Invitations began to flow in from all over England. The door was not just unlocked, it was thrown open wide, and Moody and Ira were nearly pushed through.

Carlisle. Darlington. Leicester.

Moody took each invitation with great seriousness. They could not possibly be in every place, not as long as they were wanted, but he filled their calendar quickly. In each city to which he committed, a small group of men would form to make arrangements. These men reserved halls, found housing for Moody and Ira, and handled all the financial details. Moody never requested a salary or gratuity of any kind. He and Ira took what was given.

Praise for the work in York spread, but not everyone welcomed this American team with open arms. Some churches feared Moody was after their offerings and would take up collections at each meeting. Others worried more about losing people than funding—they suspected Moody of steering his listeners between denominations.

And some mistrusted Ira. One rumor had it that he was a representative of the company that made small organs like those he used in the song services. Other criticisms centered on the texts he sang or the tunes he chose.

Moody pushed a letter toward Ira as they sat quietly one afternoon, writing and planning for the coming weeks.

"I think you'd better go ahead to Sunderland, Ira," he said.

"Sunderland? Why?"

"Look what Rees writes," Moody said, pulling the page back so he could see it again. " 'We are most interested in what we know of your ministry. Can you be the same Moody who's been in Ireland and throughout the country?' That's suspicion, Ira, definitely suspicious of us."

"I don't know. He asks for information. No harm in that is there?"

"Ira, consider. Shouldn't we attempt to forestall the penny collections drama of last month?"

That incident had nearly sent Ira home in frustration. After accepting an invitation from a town on the northern coast of England, Ira and Moody had been surprised a few days before their departure to find a delegation of ministers from the town at their door. The men had

traveled most of the morning to reach them and withdraw the invitation.

They had used many words and a fair number of in-
comprehensible shrugs and looks. But in the end their
message was simple and clear: They feared a Moody revival would draw many of their usual summer visitors,
and, with them, the "penny collections" that the churches
depended on to meet financial obligations throughout
the year.

Moody had listened to them quietly, and then, just as
quietly, accepted the withdrawn invitation.

"It is easier fighting the devil than fighting ministers,"
he said.

Ira said later that he was sorry for the town.

"They've lost an opportunity, Fanny, mark my words."

She knew he meant Moody, not himself. By that time,
they had both spent enough hours under Moody's preaching and in his presence to recognize his submission to his
Master and that Master's powerful work through him.

Ira reached for the letter, which Moody was still
holding.

"I'll go ahead," he said, "and see if I can convince
all concerned that we'll take no collections, pennies or
pounds."

Moody smiled.

"Thank you, Ira. You will do marvelously, I'm sure.
I'll meet you there by the end of the week."

The Rev. Rees, interested letter writer, met Ira at the
train station.

"Mr. Sankey, so glad you could come. I never expected
such a lively answer to my letter!"

"Yes, well, Mr. Moody asked me to come ahead and
be sure all was arranged and comfortably settled."

Ira regretted the words immediately.

"I don't mean," he added quickly, "that Mr. Moody requires any particularly gracious setting. I mean only that he is concerned, anxious that you and the other ministers are quite satisfied to have us and comfortable with our usual practices."

"Yes, of course," Rees said. "Well, now I have been wondering if your Mr. Moody could be the same Moody I met briefly in Ireland perhaps a year ago. You see, we were assigned lodging together one night, and he led in an evening devotion like nothing I have ever experienced. His prayers were . . . they were conversations with God, Mr. Sankey. And his love for the Word and his passion in preaching it, well, if this is the same man who is now your partner, I am only too eager to have him at my chapel."

Ira smiled.

"I think you and I speak of the same man," he said. "And he will be very glad to hear your concerns were centered on his identity as the same man you met a year ago."

"Could there have been other concerns?" Rees asked, confused.

"Well, before you ask, let me assure you we take no collections and," Ira felt the boldness of suspecting he spoke to a like-minded man, "we have no designs on your church's income."

Rees laughed.

"Well then! It had not entered my mind, but it is good to know. I'll tuck the information away in case I am asked by any colleagues."

Rees escorted Ira to his lodging house and asked him if an hour would be enough to settle in.

"I'd like you to dine with me and my friend Longstaff. He is our treasurer and will be greatly relieved by the news you bring."

Ira glanced up, startled, and saw Rees grinning broadly.

"In an hour then," Ira said, smiling back.

The dinner wasn't about money, Ira knew that. But it was, in fact, another kind of test, a fact he learned later. When they had finished eating, Mr. Longstaff directed them into a parlor and immediately pointed Ira to a small, American organ.

"I believe you know Mr. Philip Phillips?" Longstaff said.

Ira nodded.

"This is the instrument he used when he presented his songs here. Would you sing for us, please?"

"Certainly. Is there some particular song you'd enjoy?"

"Sing what is on your heart."

Ira settled himself in a chair and positioned his fingers above the keys. He paused only the slightest moment to offer a silent prayer. Then he sang.

"Free from the law, O happy condition, Jesus has bled and there is remission."

Rees listened quietly to that song and several others.

When Ira met Moody at the station a few days later, both were surprised to see large placards announcing their meetings: "D. L. Moody of Chicago will preach the gospel, and Ira D. Sankey of Chicago will sing the gospel in Bethesda Saturday, at 3 and 7 o'clock. All are welcome."

It was not until after they'd left Sunderland that Ira learned Rees once had been opposed to solos, organ music, and even choral presentations in his church. But that night in Longstaff's home, something changed his mind. And, to Ira's knowledge, he was the first to christen Ira's work "singing the gospel."

The label would stick for the rest of Ira's life.

He tried regularly to check his heart, recognizing an ever-present temptation to sing for the love of it and not for the love of Christ. But like Moody, he was passionate about showing men their sin and their urgent need of salvation. He was convinced music might convey the message to some who otherwise refused to listen. Many at the time agreed with him.

"The secret of Mr. Sankey's power lies not in his gift of song, but in the spirit, of which the song is only the expression. He, too, is a man in earnest and sings in the full confidence that God is working by him," theologian and author E. J. Goodspeed wrote in the late 1870s. Just like Moody, Sankey "has a message to lost men from God the Father."

The Rev. Stewart, pastor of a congregation that preferred very formal services, agreed.

"The right and duty of every layman is by precept and example to bring erring souls to Christ, and in the exercise of this plain right I bid these evangelists Godspeed in their good work of awakening souls," Stewart said.

The tunes Ira eventually wrote were simple and catchy. He had no training in composition and wrote what he liked and thought people could easily learn. His favorite songs for use in the services had refrains. Their repetitiveness made it easy for the crowd to quickly join in.

Ira made a distinction between his gospel hymns and worship hymns.

"One class is to teach and the other—such as 'Praise God from Whom All Blessings Flow' and 'Jesus, Lover of My Soul'—are hymns in which the whole congregation can praise God," he said.

The campaign grew as it continued, and soon the buildings reserved for the meetings proved to be too small. Hundreds and thousands were turned away. More meetings were added to the schedule. In Liverpool they met at Victoria Hall, a structure erected specifically for their use. It held ten thousand, and it was filled eighteen times in a week.

In London, they met in a great hall that held fourteen thousand. For five weeks they held services twice each day but Saturday.

"Blind, indeed, must that man be who fails to discern in all this the mighty power of that same Holy Spirit who rested on the apostles on that memorable day," reporter John Lobb wrote in his book on the meetings, comparing them to Pentecost.

Even so, detractors remained. One London satirist published a lively paper he called "The Moody and Sankey Humbug."

He sold thousands of copies to the crowds flooding into the meetings and soon ran out. Something—he would later say the Holy Spirit—prompted him to step inside and collect some fresh, first-hand material for a next edition of his paper.

"He went out, not to write a paper but to destroy his paper that he had written and so tell what the Holy Ghost had done for him," Lobb wrote.

12

"We Will Offer Our Tribute of Praise"

The singing in the services was still best when Ira led tunes the congregation knew. But more often now he began a hymn with a tune from across the ocean and soon heard other voices raised with his.

He delighted in learning new songs and passing them on to the people.

He first sang "In the Sweet By and By" and "Christ Arose" in Newcastle. By the end of the week, he could hear both at the rail station, while passing the shipyards, and even when walking below an open apartment window.

Ira was amazed each time he sang that the words could minister as fervently to others as they did to his own heart.

"There's a land that is fairer than day, and by faith we can see it afar," he sang one night.

The first verse was no problem, but his voice, known so well now for its strength, broke at the third.

"To our bountiful Father above, we will offer our tribute of praise for the glorious gift of His love and the blessings that hallow our days."

The song was in great demand. As the meetings in Newcastle filled to overflowing, the people were sent out to nearby chapels and halls. Prayer meetings were held, and Moody and Ira would circulate between the sites. Some folks chose to follow Ira from place to place, to hear this song and others repeatedly and, hopefully, learn some of the words for themselves.

Two weeks into the meetings at Newcastle, Ira noticed he no longer sang "In the Sweet By and By" as a solo. Lips moved around the hall, and some could even be heard singing along softly. He could hardly wait to speak to Fanny when the service ended, but many people came up the aisles that night, seeking counsel and partners in prayer.

It wasn't until they were walking back to their hotel that he finally could share his idea.

"Fanny, I think we should start up a choir," Ira said.

She slowed her pace just a fraction and looked at him in surprise.

"A choir? Who do you propose to have sing?"

"The people, Fanny. I wish you could share my view when I sing each night. They are there, all through the crowd, singing with me, mouthing as many words as they've already learned. I think it would be a real help in bringing these songs home to their congregations and what's more, I think they'd like it!"

She laughed then.

"Oh, Ira, you'd make them like it. I can hear that in your voice."

"You don't really care for the idea, though, do you?" he said.

"Yes. Yes, I do," Fanny said. "You mistake me. I'm just enjoying your enthusiasm for this bold new project."

"It can be done, Fanny. I've thought it out—we'll assemble thirty minutes, maybe forty, before each service, and we'll sing the songs they like best, the new ones that they want to know. I'll give them the texts. It will be real help when we attempt to sing the songs as a full body if many of the people already know them."

"You have thought this out, haven't you?"

"You'll join, won't you? I'll need some others who already know the songs."

"Do you really have to ask, Ira?"

His hand was lightly supporting her elbow and he squeezed it for a moment.

"I don't deserve you," he said.

"Nor I you," Fanny answered. "So we must both thank our Father daily."

The choir was announced at the following night's service. Ira had scarcely eaten that day. He had been up half the night before, agonizing over which songs would be most appropriate for this use. His decisions made, he'd rushed to the printer to have copies made.

"Will two dozen do, do you think?" he asked Fanny as they waited for the printer to finish his notes on the order.

"Better make it three," she said.

The printer looked up with a question on his face.

"Three," Ira said. "Three dozen."

"Yes, sir. They'll be ready in two days," the printer said.

"Fine, fine. Thank you for rushing this."

Two nights later, Ira passed out the neatly folded sheets, each of which bore the words for six songs. They weren't much, from a publishing perspective. But they opened the door to let in the project for which Ira would become known worldwide.

Ira's notebook of songs and poems was beginning to show significant signs of wear. He carried it with him constantly, wanting it at the ready if he found new material and wanting to be always ready himself when a song was in need.

As his unfamiliar solos became more popular, Ira's book began to be in great demand. Choir directors begged for a chance to borrow it.

"Just until the morning," one said. "I will copy down all I can in the night and have it back to you first thing tomorrow."

Another asked Ira for a few pages, saying he'd like more when he brought these back.

Ira did not travel far down this road before he found himself at a meeting, standing to sing without his book. While he knew most of the tunes by heart, he was nervous to rely on his memory for the texts.

Ira and Fanny returned to the print shop. Ira carried his notebook and, in the front, clean copies of the texts for eight songs people requested most often.

He arranged to have the words printed on small cards, so he could hand them out to those who asked.

Fanny brought a packet in her handbag the same evening they were delivered. She was at Ira's side after the service, when, as usual, some approached him about the songs.

"Mr. Sankey, that solo blessed my heart, and I know it would do my dear mother much good as well. I don't suppose you—"

Fanny leaned across her husband, a card in hand.

"Here," she said. "Here it is. May God minister to your heart through it as He has to ours."

"Thank you, ma'am," he said.

By the time the fifth person in line approached the Sankeys, the addresses were being made to Fanny and her neat stack of cards.

"I'll have one of those, please," said a woman who obviously had been crying. "Thank you so much."

Fanny looked up and saw a line of people forming in the aisle and reaching back to the entryway. She glanced

down at the stack in her hands, which suddenly seemed meager.

The cards were gone that night.

Ira reported the results to Moody over a late dinner and was surprised when his colleague laughed.

"Of course you ran out, Sankey," he said. "The songs grab hearts; they can have the words for free. It was an excellent plan."

"But I don't think it's a plan that can endure," Ira said. "I cannot afford it to endure!"

Moody laughed again.

"We'll think of some way to get these songs to the masses, Sankey. What about putting them in their hymnbooks? Might take a while, but then there they'd be to stay."

Ira promised to look into it.

They were using *Hallowed Songs* in their services, but the hymnal contained very few of the solos the people loved. Ira wrote to the publisher to see about having the most popular songs bound into the back of the next edition. He received a letter in response almost immediately.

"Regrettably, sir, we are unable to alter the book for future editions without express permission from Mr. Philip Phillips, who prepared the book for publication. Sincerely yours . . ."

"Phillips!" said Fanny. "Surely he would be agreeable. You must write back immediately and tell them you're a friend of Phillips."

The second letter had no more impact than the first. But Ira would not throw the idea away. He had seen the hunger for these songs, had sensed the balm of the gospel set to music. He paid for another stack of cards that Fanny could pass out judiciously. And he began to write, letter after letter, to publishers and musicians and any contact he could think of.

The more refusals he got, the more agitated he became. His frustration spilled out during a dinner when R.C. Morgan, editor of London's journal *The Christian*, was visiting to prepare his report on Moody's meetings. Morgan and Moody were sipping coffee and discussing the spiritual merits of smaller prayer meetings versus mass meetings.

"I do think there is benefit in each man being able to speak to God, in the presence of others," Moody said. "So few have the opportunity when we meet in such large groups."

"Yes, but to learn from the hearts of others, to learn from you, Moody, how to address the Father, is a lesson they won't get otherwise," Morgan said. "We cannot limit the impact."

Ira broke in.

"Really, Mr. Morgan, there's no need to debate further, as we all know you British are so set in your ways there's no real chance we'll convince anyone that house meetings would serve as effectively for prayer as our daily gathering."

Morgan looked puzzled, but Moody laughed.

"Mr. Sankey has a knack for bringing the conversation around to this," he said. "You'll have to hear him out now, Morgan."

Ira felt heat in his neck and cheeks.

"Forgive me, sir, I know I sounded petulant," he said. "I admit my mind is much occupied now with the resistance I'm meeting among your countrymen."

"What are they resisting, Mr. Sankey? Are we still speaking of prayer meetings?"

"No, no—though they are not interested in that idea either," Ira said, smiling himself now. "I have been attempting to give the people some songs, just a few songs, the ones they most seem to love and which touch their hearts. But I can find no one to take them, despite my willingness to submit them at no charge. I have come to the conclusion it is true that England is unbending to a fault!"

"Mr. Sankey, you have, at last, made your case to the right person," Morgan said.

"I don't understand," Ira said.

"I don't just print a newspaper, sir. I have for years been printing music leaflets, and I would be honored to take on this task of yours—if only to show you not all Englishmen are unwilling to try something new."

Morgan laughed, and Ira joined him. Moody looked greatly satisfied and smiled as he raised his coffee again.

When Morgan returned to London, he carried with him twenty-three texts that Ira had copied from his scrapbook. They were rolled together, and Ira wrote carefully on the curved surface: "Sacred Songs and Solos, sung by Ira D. Sankey at the meetings of Mr. Moody of Chicago."

In two weeks, the pamphlets were ready. The first five hundred copies were sold for sixpence each and were gone within a day. The second printing was snatched up as quickly and within weeks Morgan was selling them in bookstores, groceries, and other markets.

Ira was in a London bookstore in 1874 when a man in sailor's attire pushed past him and hurried to the counter.

"Give me a dozen little Sankeys, quick," he said.

So much for the name Ira had labored over.

The Princess of Wales herself had a copy. Ira presented it to her personally when she and some other members of the royal family attended meetings in London. The Duchess of Sutherland told him later that the princess enjoyed gathering her children with her around the piano and singing from the little book.

The pamphlet that Morgan flooded across England eventually became one of the most widely printed and used hymnbooks in the world. At its peak, it contained about twelve hundred pieces.

Even songs that weren't Ira's work bore his mark. More than once he changed the words of another poet to make them fresher or somehow easier to sing.

The Rev. John Stockton wrote "Come Every Soul by Sin Oppressed" with this chorus: "Come to Jesus, come to Jesus, come to Jesus just now."

Ira changed the phrase to: "Only trust Him, only trust Him, only trust Him now. He will save you, He will save you, He will save you now."

He felt no compunction about changing pieces repeatedly, even after they were in print. He rarely left the final chorus of this particular song alone, sometimes having the congregation sing "I will trust Him" and other times "I do trust Him."

He made a similar change to a text by F. H. Rawley, replacing "Can't you sing the wondrous story" with "I will sing the wondrous story."

Over the years Ira worried about having his hand in too many songs. Sometimes he wrote under the name Rian A. Dykes. The anagram of his name might have fooled only a few, but it made him feel better.

Within a matter of years *Sacred Songs and Solos* was so popular that royalties from it provided enough money to construct the first buildings for the school Moody founded at Northfield.

The idea had been born during a visit to Massachusetts. Moody was visiting the poor in the mountains near his childhood home. At one sad farm he met a woman who, with her daughters, was making straw hats to support the family while her husband was sick in bed.

Moody could not comprehend how they planned to survive. The farm was too meager to support them much longer even if the father regained his health. The two girls told him they would love to go to school and be educated and find some better way to support the family. An idea was planted in Moody's head, and he could not let it go.

He saw Ira soon after that visit.

"I have made up my mind to start a school for the poor girls in New England," he said.

The school was an idea under development for some years as Moody and Ira traveled and ministered in Great Britain.

When *Sacred Songs and Solos* met with wide acclaim, Ira began to consider what to do with the money he was earning. He and Moody were careful to take only what was needed as pay and were hesitant to become even moderately wealthy from these songbooks that they considered the Lord's work.

"I think the money from your hymnbook would be just the thing to get my school started when we are back home, Ira," Moody announced suddenly one morning. "I have been thinking this over for some time, and I believe it's the answer we've been seeking."

Ira did not hesitate.

In 1879 Northfield Seminary for Young Ladies was founded, and two years later Mount Hermon School for Boys.

These were not Moody's only contributions to education. In the 1880s he began the Moody Bible Institute in the city he loved. There, students were taught Bible study methods and evangelism. Graduates went on to become pastors, evangelists, missionaries, music ministers, and Sunday school teachers.

And Ira's home was not forgotten either. The proceeds from *Sacred Songs and Solos* were sufficient to allow Ira to give a gift to the agency that had led him to Moody and the Chicago work.

In 1886 he attended the dedication of the New Castle YMCA, complete with a gym, reading rooms, school rooms, an art gallery, and large halls for group meetings.

Almost as much as Ira loved sharing music with others, he loved sharing stories attached to the music. As the first British campaign moved forward, he took notes to remind himself of hearts that had been touched by a certain song or a text that met a deep need for a hurting believer.

As his music collection grew, so did his notes and stories. He researched the lives of the great hymn writers and wrote short essays on their best-loved hymns. Eventually, this work would turn into another Sankey book—this time, one to read, not to sing.

13

"Christ Hath Redeemed Us Once for All"

Ira and Moody were becoming accustomed to England—and it to them.

The welcomes of well-known conservative pastors, the hearty approval of the "little Sankey" books, even the growing acceptance of the organ were reaching new cities before they did.

But in November 1873, as the weather turned bitter, Ira feared their reception would do the same. They were headed for Scotland.

Scottish theologians and scholars published and spoke eloquently against the organ, or, as they called it, the "kist o'whistles," an expression uttered with obvious distaste. It was the same phrase used for someone who took wheezy, noisy breaths.

Some critics openly argued that Moody and Ira had come to Great Britain because they and their message were unwelcome in their own country. Hearing this, thirty pastors and laymen from Chicago drafted a statement of support which they sent for publication in the Edinburgh papers.

Fanny reminded Ira how minds had been changed in England. Together they prayed that he would choose the proper songs and sing them earnestly and well, pointing souls only to the cross, never to the man singing of it.

Ira and Moody disliked the formal receptions they sometimes met when arriving in new cities. They had begun to make a habit of entering a place unannounced. And so they slipped into Edinburgh without any notice and settled into a hotel in the center of the city.

Ira was stiff and sluggish after their journey. He left his unpacked bags against a wall and headed back to the street for a walk. He had not gone half a block when someone stopped him.

"Ah, Mr. Sankey. Is this you?" asked a stranger. "When did you arrive, and where is Mr. Moody?"

Ira was startled but admitted to being himself. The man who'd found him in the sea of faces was the head of the welcoming committee . . . and had been watching for them for days. He was appalled to learn the men had checked into a hotel.

"Not at all," he said. "That won't do. We've arranged comfortable, private housing for you. Come, let's collect Mr. Moody and get you properly settled."

The home to which he brought them was lovely. Large and comfortably furnished, it was a place where they could rest thoroughly and well.

Ira lost some of his nervousness about their Scottish reception. In fact, he was so at ease those first days in the city that he set himself to a task he'd been planning for some time.

In England he'd been singing a text by Alfred, Lord Tennyson.

"Late, late, so late! and dark the night and chill, Late, late, so late! but we can enter still."

But when he wrote asking permission to include the copyrighted words in the first edition of *Sacred Songs*, he was firmly rebuffed. Ira loved the image of the late hour that still held a welcome for one more repentant soul. He asked Horatius Bonar, a Scottish pastor and hymn writer, to capture the idea in a new poem that Ira could set to music.

Bonar sent him "Yet There is Room," which included this passage: "O enter in; that banquet is for thee; that cup of everlasting joy is free; room, room, still room! O enter, enter now."

In that quiet room in Scotland, Ira made his first formal attempt at setting a text to music. It would not be his last.

Despite the warm welcome in an Edinburgh home and the propitious beginning of a new song, an evil spirit appeared to be at work to derail those opening meetings in Scotland.

The first meeting was scheduled for Sunday, November 23. It had been announced for days and long before the appointed hour, the hall was filled. Some reports said two thousand were turned away.

A local minister opened the service with disappointing news: Mr. Moody of Chicago had become ill while en route from England and would be unable to attend that evening. However, Mr. Sankey still was able to sing, and the Rev. J. H. Wilson was prepared and eager to preach the Word.

Ira could feel the letdown in the room. Doubt crept in and told him he would add to it. After an opening prayer, he led the crowd in singing Psalm 100.

A Bible reading followed, and then another prayer.

The time had come for Ira's solo. He had thought and prayed long over his choice.

"Ho! all ye heavy laden, come! Here's pardon, comfort, rest and home: Ye wand'rers from a Father's face, return, accept His proffered grace; ye tempted ones, there's refuge nigh: Jesus of Nazareth passeth by."

The packed room was unnaturally quiet. Ira would not allow himself to think about why or worry about their impressions.

"But if you still His call refuse, and all His wondrous love abuse, soon will He sadly from you turn, your bitter prayer for pardon spurn, 'Too late! too late!' will be the cry—Jesus of Nazareth has passed by."
He moved quickly to his seat but not before noticing the thoughtful expressions on some faces and the tears in a few eyes. When Ira rose for a closing solo, he chose a piece in which he always asked the congregation to join him on the chorus.

"Hold the fort, for I am coming," he sang, and each time he reached the chorus more voices throughout the hall joined him. Ira's fears were put to rest. But the difficult spirit remained at work to disturb the meetings.

Moody presided over the second service alone as Ira had the first. The organ had been forgotten, and the men called upon to deliver it at the last moment had an accident and spilled the instrument into the street. It was damaged beyond use.

The next morning, Ira read an unsigned opinion in Edinburgh's leading newspaper: "Clearly something powerful is at work to break up any scheme these two men of Chicago may have for working together in our midst." He tried not to sigh at the satisfied tone.

Putting their first two nights behind them, Ira and Moody prepared to jointly lead the services that third night.

Ira sat down at the organ as the hall filled. After the previous night's disaster, the committee had scoured the county for a replacement instrument. Glancing out into the faces before him, Ira was startled to see one looking intently back at him.

The older man smiled and nodded slightly. Ira nodded too, and then looked quickly for someone he knew who might also know this man in the front row. He was relieved when a member of the planning committee approached him to discuss the order of the service.

"Can you tell me, who is that man, there, just at this end of the front row?"

"I think you must mean Dr. Bonar."

"Dr. Bonar? Horatius Bonar?"

"Yes, the poet."

"Thank you," Ira said. His voice sounded weak in his own ears.

This man wrote those compelling words Ira had set to music just days before. Many considered him one of the greatest hymn writers of the day.

"I came to Jesus as I was, so weary, worn, and sad; I found in Him a resting place, and He has made me glad," Bonar had written.

Ira thought Bonar's work was beautiful and worshipful. The anxiety he had set aside earlier came rushing back. But Ira determined not to be sucked into the fears of a performer.

He stood at the appointed time for his solo. But before he sang, he asked the congregation to join him in prayer.

"Dear Father," Ira said. "I wish to be a blessing, a spiritual blessing, to these dear people gathered tonight to know you better. Will you hide me and shine your light on the truths of which I sing? I ask not for a strong voice or a tuneful presentation but only that your great salvation would declare itself to us. Amen."

His fear slipped away and he sang.

"Free from the law, oh, happy condition, Jesus has bled and there is remission."

And his voice was strong and it was tuneful as he shared the words by his friend Philip Bliss, words he believed utterly.

"Cling to the cross, the burden will fall, Christ hath redeemed us once for all."

Bonar was smiling as Ira sat down. When the service ended, he came to Ira quickly and held out his hand.

"Well, Mr. Sankey," he said, gripping the younger man's hand. "And so you sang the gospel tonight."

"I hope I did, sir," Ira said. "I know that's all I mean to do, but I fear Ira Sankey sometimes gets in the way of the message."

"He did not tonight, sir," Bonar said. "And I trust he will scarcely at all as the days go by."

"Dr. Bonar, I've set 'Yet There is Room' to music this very week. May I bring you a copy tomorrow night?"

"Thank you, Mr. Sankey. I would like that very much."

Ira promised to bring the piece the following evening, if he had to stay up all night to copy it. And Bonar, for his part, wrote a letter of support for Moody and Sankey that was meant to be personal but soon was widely distributed.

"These men have the most definite of all definite aims—winning souls to everlasting joy," he said. "And they look for no fame and no reward save the Master's approval."

From that night on Ira struggled little with fears before he sang. When he stood and felt the slightest urge to surrender to anxiety or self-consciousness, he remembered Bonar's quiet reassurance: Ira Sankey was not in the way that night and may not be at all in the future.

One night in Edinburgh, a woman waited patiently for a conversation with Ira after the service. He shook her hand warmly and thanked her for coming.

"No, sir, it's you I've come to thank," she said. "Your dear song, 'Safe in the Arms of Jesus' means more to this old soul than you can know."

"I can say how glad I am to hear that with no fear of pride," Ira answered. "That is not my song, madam. You have mistaken me for a gifted poet, my friend Fanny Crosby."

"Surely you've sung it? I know I heard it not two nights ago."

"Oh, yes, I sing it and many of her other songs gladly. She has a gift for lifting eyes and hearts to the Savior. But I had no hand in that lovely piece. Do you know anything of Miss Crosby?"

Ira and Crosby had been friends for some years already, connected by their mutual love of music and its power to influence hearts for Christ. He and Fanny had spent many happy hours with Crosby and her husband, Alexander Van Alstyne, or Van, as friends called him.

Ira shared Crosby's story at the front of that church in Edinburgh: Blind at six weeks, running from God, and then finally submissive to Him.

"And not just submissive, but rejoicing," Ira said. "I know that sounds impossible. I wish you could hear her say it herself. She would tell you, 'It was no doctor's mistake that left me blind. It was the direct and completed plan of God to take my physical vision and prepare me for a grander vision of His great love. If I had my sight, I would not be so suited to help others see Him.' "

He laughed.

"But she would say it much more beautifully than I."

"You do your friend justice, Mr. Sankey, I assure you. When you go on back to America, give her my love and tell her an old Scots woman sends her blessing."

Ira did introduce one of his own hymn tunes on a follow-up visit to Edinburgh—"The Ninety and Nine." It became, arguably, the best-known and best-loved of his works in his lifetime.

Ira considered the song a gift from God, granted to a servant who had done nothing more than collect clippings for years, waiting for the time when they might be put to profitable use.

Any skeptic would call the circumstances pure chance. Ira and Moody had been at the Glasgow train station en route to Edinburgh for three days of meetings—a brief follow-up to the three months they'd already spent in that city. All through their European travels, Ira was starved for news from America. His newspaper habits, formed when he was still a boy, had grown only stronger in adulthood.

That day, just before they boarded their train, he passed a penny to a newsboy and took from him a slim weekly paper.

The pages held no solace for a man feeling pangs for home. He found only a reprinted sermon by a fellow American—nothing to satisfy his need for news.

Ira set the paper aside and tried to rest. But he wasn't as tired as he thought. Shortly, he picked up the paper again and began to browse the advertisements.

A poem, nestled into one corner, caught his eye: "The Ninety and Nine," by Elizabeth Clephane.

Its words struck Ira as he read it once, then again.

"This would be a marvelous gospel song, Mr. Moody," he said.

"Hmmm?"

"This, this poem," Ira said, holding out the newspaper.

"Will you read it to me?" Moody said.

Ira did so. And though it was only his third reading, he invested in it the enthusiasm that seemed suitable for each passage and was, in fact, quite satisfied with his delivery.

He looked at Moody for his response and found his friend deep in a letter. He didn't even notice Ira had stopped speaking.

Ira did not press him. He clipped the piece neatly from the page and tucked it into his notebook, determined to return to it, and soon.

On the second day of those Edinburgh meetings, he had his chance. Moody and several others had preached a series of sermons from John 10, in which Jesus identifies himself as the Good Shepherd. When the last speaker was finished, Moody turned to Ira.

"Have you a solo appropriate for this subject, with which to close the service?"

Ira usually was prepared for the question, but that day he felt strangely uncertain. The Twenty-third Psalm would fit, but they had sung it several times already in these meetings. And it was such a favorite that Ira knew the moment he began to sing it, he would be joined by most of the crowd. It would not be the thoughtful, piercing solo he was sure Moody wanted.

It seemed another mind spoke to his: The new poem.

Impossible, he thought, *I have no tune for it.*

But he could not shake the idea. The words were beautiful and could not be more appropriate. He opened his notebook and found the slip he'd removed from the newspaper so recently.

Father, let me sing so people will hear and understand, he prayed silently.

Then he gave himself an A-flat chord and began to sing.

"There were ninety and nine that safely lay in the shelter of the fold; but one was out on the hills away, far off from the gates of gold. Away on the mountains wild and bare; away from the tender Shepherd's care."

He sang slowly, each note following naturally on the one before it. And he did not struggle to recall the tune for the second stanza.

"Although the road be rough and steep, I go to the desert to find My sheep."

The room was still as he sang the third and fourth stanzas. Ira finished the last line of the fifth, and final, stanza—"Rejoice, for the Lord brings back His own!"—then heard a sigh sweep through the room.

Moody went to Ira instead of to the pulpit as everyone expected. As he approached, Ira could see tears in his eyes.

"Sankey, where did you get that hymn?" Moody said. "I never heard the like of it in my life."

"It is the hymn I read to you yesterday on the train," Ira said. "I know you did not hear it, but I was certain you would appreciate it."

Moody nodded. "Indeed," he said. "Indeed, I do."

He straightened and would have quieted the crowd, but it was not necessary. No one spoke.

"Let us pray," Moody said.

The meeting ended, but the life of "The Ninety and Nine" had only begun.

On the whole, Ira and his organ slipped easily into Scottish and Irish sacred society. Newspapers grudgingly offered their opinions that a simple organ, for the purpose of keeping a song on tune, was "no hindrance to the devout and spiritual worship of God."

Dublin's Exhibition Palace, which held more than ten thousand, was filled every night. These thousands didn't come to see men of impressive rank or wealth. They had been told not to expect masterful oratory. Moody's preaching did not rank among greatness for those who evaluated such things. But they expected—and found—Christ lifted up and His Word proclaimed plainly and fearlessly.

And these things were true of Ira's songs as well. Rustling and whispers grew quiet when he stepped to the podium. The *Irish Times* reported that when he sings "it seems that he only is present in the vast building."

One night an elderly gentleman waited to speak to Ira in the inquiry room. Other men finished their conversations and gladly would have spoken with him. But it had to be Mr. Sankey, he said.

Ira shook the man's hand and asked him to sit down.

"How may I pray with you, sir?"

"You will be disappointed to know me, Mr. Sankey," the man said. "Until last night, I was utterly careless about my soul and what eternity might hold for me. But I have been so unhappy since last night, I could not sleep. I seemed to hear ringing in my ears, 'Jesus of Nazareth is passing by,' and if I don't get saved now, I never shall be."

A single tear coursed down his cheek as he looked into Ira's eyes.

"Is it not too late for me? It is possible He has not passed by completely?"

"Oh, no. It is not too late," Ira said. "He has called you, and He waits now for your answer. There will be joy in heaven when you say yes."

The Rev. E. J. Goodspeed was with Moody and Ira through most of their first trip to Great Britain and wrote at length about the meetings shortly after they returned home.

"The singing of Mr. Sankey lays the gospel message and invitation very distinctly and powerfully on the consciences of the people," he said. "I have never found it objected to except by those who have not witnessed it. Those who have come and heard have departed with their prejudices vanquished and their hearts impressed."

Lives were changed, and the gospel spread as those who'd experienced its joy could not keep silent. Sometimes groups of thirty or forty would meet in one of the small towns or at some quiet country train station and come into the city for a service.

Ira loved to hear later that their return trips were filled with music, including some of the songs they had just learned, and that they often shared the gospel with those on the train with them.

Ira and Fanny rejoiced privately as well when David Sankey arrived in Scotland shortly after the new year with their two sons in tow. These were happy days for the little family, reunited after so many months.

"Listen to this," Moody said one evening, waving an unfolded page toward Ira and Fanny. "A young woman died in Glasgow of the scarlet fever. Her father writes to tell us this: 'Her departure, however, has been singularly softened to us, for she told us yesterday she was going home to be with Jesus. She told us to let Mr. Moody and Mr. Sankey know that she died a happy Christian.' "

Fanny could not hear such reports without being affected. Her cheeks were flushed and her eyes damp.

"Praise be to God," she said.

"That pays us for crossing the Atlantic, I should think, Sankey," Moody said.

"Undoubtedly."

Crowds gathered when Moody and Sankey left a country, just as when they arrived. Moody said a few words as they bid Scotland farewell, but closed just as he did when services ended in a city. No "good-bye" or "farewell" for him.

"Good night," he said. "And meet us in the morning."

And he pointed to the sky.

14
"Come Home, O Prodigal"

In two years and hundreds of services, Ira had numerous opportunities to see astonishing responses as God worked in people's hearts while Moody preached.

He thought often of the Rev. Rees's phrase, "singing the gospel." The idea reminded him of the urgency of his work and renewed his conviction that people must hear the words at all costs. With every note—sometimes speaking more than singing—he urged people to consider eternity and the One who died to save them.

His solos were a near-seamless extension of Moody's sermons.

"Come home, O prodigal, come home," Ira sang one night in Sunderland.

The hall was silent as the last note faded, then, in the hush, everyone clearly heard a young man's voice: "Father, will you forgive me?"

The speaker rushed from the back of the hall to the seat of a man who must have been his father. They embraced and both wept.

"My boy, I forgive everything," the older man said. "Let us go together and ask God to forgive us both."

Onlookers were respectfully silent as the pair left for a prayer room, but once they were gone, a movement spread through the crowd. Hundreds rose and followed toward the adjoining rooms, which soon were bursting.

The experience was uncannily similar to the breakthrough in York, where one pastor's humble repentance broke the resistance of a city.

Ira could not sleep that night. He lay awake, reviewing the service in his mind. The impact of one penitent man was beyond anything he would have predicted. The responsibility to lead others in the straight, narrow way or the wide, bending way was in each man's hands. It was in his hands.

"Father," Ira whispered into the dark. "Father, forgive me for the songs I've sung for the people and not for You. I am a wretched man, but You put me before these other men to set an example, and with Your help I will set it. Let the first prodigal to return every night be me."

Ira and Moody both kept notes and journals of the people they met and spoke to during the meetings in Europe.

One Saturday evening Ira recorded an encounter in a gypsy camp in Epping Forest near London. Some of the men, leaders in the camp, had been won to Christ and now were sharing the gospel in their circle. While Moody spent time praying with them and encouraging them in their work, Ira sat in the carriage, observing the activity in the camp.

He had not known what to expect that morning when Moody announced their destination. Gypsies generated both interest and revulsion with their unorthodox ways of living. They made wagons and tents their homes and always were on the move, an impossible life for most people to understand. But they were not shunned. Their handmade baskets and finely bred horses were as good as money and were in great demand.

By the late 1880s the band that spent much of its time in Epping Forest was on regular display. The gypsies charged admission, and thousands paid to see their camps and watch them work. Most of all, they came for the balls. Dusk would fall, and the gypsies would hang lamps from poles across an open field. A hired band played long into the night, and visitors swirled and stomped alongside the gypsies, dancing until every blade of grass had been crushed beneath thousands of feet.

But Ira visited earlier in the group's history and saw a circle of tents and a scene that was, on the whole, quieter than he expected. Women in vibrant dresses were making baskets. Some of the men were tending to horses staked just back of the vans that formed a wall behind the living area.

Some of the younger boys came up to Ira's side, their dark eyes staring at him, unblinking. He felt uncomfortable, but decided he ought to smile. A boy who could have been thirteen or fourteen smiled back.

"Do you know what Mr. Moody has come to talk of with your elders?"

Ira could have been asking the whole group, but he was looking at the boy who smiled.

"We know, sir," the boy answered.

"Yes?" Ira said.

"Of Jesus and that Bible and those meetings in the big halls in the city. My father's been right impressed by it all."

Ira no longer pretended to be talking to all of them.

"Do you understand it, lad? Do you know your own need when they speak of it?"

"Not sure that I do, sir, though my father wishes I might."

Moody was suddenly ready to leave, and Ira had to end the conversation abruptly.

"May the Lord make a preacher of you, my boy!" he said, laying his hand briefly on the boy's head before they drove away.

The boy smiled once more but said nothing else.

The two would meet again fifteen years later, when the young preacher, Gypsy Smith, made his first trip to America for evangelistic meetings. Ira took the younger man for a drive in Brooklyn, unaware that this was not their first meeting. Smith reminded him of the brief Saturday visit to the camp years before, and of his parting words to a smiling boy.

"I am that boy," he said.

Ira's joy tumbled out in a great laugh.

———————————

After the meetings Ira often had opportunities to pray with men who came to the inquiry rooms for counsel. They sometimes arrived with tears in their eyes, as Moody's preaching helped them first understand the depth of their own sin.

On other occasions the messages in Ira's songs prodded people to decisions. Goodspeed considered them the perfect partners.

"The special gifts of each evangelist have been most happily wedded together for the common purpose they have in view," he said.

In Scotland one night a man who appeared to be drunk loudly entered the hall as Moody preached. He made a fair disturbance as he settled into a seat and had hardly quieted down when he stood up again.

"Mr. Moody, will you please stop a bit, I want to hear Mr. Sankey sing 'The Ninety and Nine,' " he said.

A few in the crowd smirked and many more frowned.

But Moody was gracious.

"All right," he said. "Sit down, my friend. I will ask Mr. Sankey to sing for you."

The organist hurried to the small instrument at the back of the platform, and Ira stood up at the pulpit.

"There were ninety and nine that safely lay in the shelter of the fold. But one was out on the hills away far off from the gates of gold. Away on the mountains wild and bare, away from the tender Shepherd's care."

Ira sang all five verses, and the man sat quietly throughout. His face did not soften, but he twisted his dirty hat in his hands over and over.

When Ira was finished, Moody stepped back up and began where he'd stopped, as if nothing unusual had happened.

At the end of the service, the man who'd asked for the song was among those who came to the inquiry room. Ira had been watching for him.

"I am so glad for a chance to talk with you, sir," he said.

"I don't know why, Mr. Sankey. I'm the black sheep of my family. Black and lost too, no doubt. Unlikely to find my way back either, thanks to the wretched bottle which I love like a child and hate with all that's in me."

"It does not have to control you any more, my friend."

"You reckon I'm the one he's searching for tonight?"

"Do you believe that?"

"Give me a paper. I want to sign my name to say I'm done drinking for good."

Ira looked at him for a moment.

"We can find a slip of paper, sir, but it will take more than a pledge to change your heart. The Shepherd doesn't want to save you just from drink. He wants to rescue you from every sin, free you from every entrapment, and put you on the path of righteousness."

The man signed his paper that night. But first, he bowed his head with Ira and asked the Lord to make him a new man.

Ira rejoiced to see him come into the meeting the next night, quietly and on time, and each night after that. They exchanged letters regularly for a year.

Many who came to the meetings said later that they had never heard the gospel explained as simply as Moody explained it.

"In not a few instances, too, Mr. Sankey's beautiful and touching solos, especially 'Jesus of Nazareth Passeth By,' 'Almost Persuaded,' and 'Prodigal Child' have proved to be arrows of conviction, entering the heart in the most unexpected manner and leading to conversion," Goodspeed wrote.

15

"Blood-drops . . . Shed for One Who Had Gone Astray"

In spring and summer of 1875, Ira and Moody traveled regularly between meetings in England and Scotland.

Then in August, after two years away, they boarded ship and set off for home.

John Lobb published a book-length account of their European work less than a year later.

"The religious movement, conducted by Messrs. Moody and Sankey in the chief cities of Great Britain and Ireland during the years 1873, 4, and 5, in many respects stands unparalleled in the history of revivals, and their visit will long be held in grateful and loving remembrance by thousands," he wrote.

Indeed, as the British ship *Spain* slid away from the dock that Tuesday in 1875, Moody and Ira waved to a vast crowd below, gathered to bid them farewell. Ira heard strains of singing as the ship passed completely away from land. He heard songs that he had sung for the first time two years ago to stoic faces and with not a voice to join him. And the song rose in his heart.

"Yes, we'll gather at the river, the beautiful, the beautiful river; gather with the saints at the river that flows by the throne of God."

Once again Ira was quite comfortable on the trip. The *Spain* accommodated one thousand four hundred passengers, and he counted himself among the happiest. On fine days he spent a great deal of time on deck, enjoying the wind from the ocean and the ship's progress. On wet days he passed the hours organizing his notes and rereading letters.

He also enjoyed long evenings rocking Ira Allen, his infant son, who had been born in Scotland. Holding the baby, who was called Allen, Ira thought he might burst in anticipation of seeing Harry and Eddie again.

Moody, the more seasoned traveler, still didn't have Ira's sea legs. But neither did he fare as badly as he had on the way over. When he was well, they spent time huddled over letters and calendars, making the same preparations they'd made for the past two years.

But this time, they would be home.

Even before they began to cross the Atlantic, Moody had called Ira away from his packing to make plans.

"I have a letter here from Northfield, Sankey."

Already interested, Ira reached for the paper Moody held toward him. Moody's birthplace was Northfield, Massachusetts. He'd been reared there with eight siblings by his widowed mother. His father had died when Moody was just four years old.

It had been a poor, quiet childhood, but his mother had faithfully ensured her children learned the ways of God. She brought them regularly to church, where they'd taken part in Sunday school and worship services.

Ultimately, with the help of the hymnal proceeds, Moody founded his two schools in Northfield. They were institutions dedicated to offering quality education and instruction in the Christian faith to those who had been denied such training because of finances or other hurdles. But in 1875, before either school was founded,

Northfield held only the appeal of home. It was a powerful draw.

Ira read the letter, then handed it back to his friend.

"Will you join me?" Moody asked.

"I would not dream of saying no," Ira said.

"Northfield will appreciate you, Sankey."

"I hope it appreciates the gospel, Mr. Moody."

Both men smiled.

They wasted little time reacquainting themselves with their homeland. Scarcely five weeks after their ship left Liverpool, Ira and Moody arrived at Northfield. Moody planned to give another of his shepherd sermons, this time focusing on the lost sheep in Luke 15, and Ira was to sing "The Ninety and Nine." It would be the song's introduction in a new country.

Arrangements had been made to use the old Congregational church, the largest sanctuary in town. But as they reached the building, they quickly saw it was overflowing.

In fact, there were more people outside the church than in it. Moody made a joke about always speaking to the largest crowd, but Ira knew it was not all jest. His friend soon was making arrangements to bring those inside out of doors.

"I will speak from the front steps of the church," he said.

While the crowd shifted, a few men carried a small cabinet organ from the sanctuary to the landing above the steps. It was a tight fit and Ira, who was not a small man, had just enough room to be seated behind it.

The outdoor audience sang well and enthusiastically. Ira felt the welcome in the people's voices and saw it on their faces. It was perhaps the most amiable crowd before which he'd stood.

He did not know that a less welcoming spirit was just across the river on the front porch of a home.

Many walking to the service that day had stopped by his home with a greeting.

"Not coming, Caldwell?" one man said. "I'm sure this would be worth your time."

"I very much doubt that," Mr. Caldwell said.

But the meeting came to him. The acoustics were surprisingly good, and Ira's voice particularly strong.

Caldwell could not help hearing.

"Lord, whence are those blood-drops all the way, that mark out the mountain's track? They were shed for one who had gone astray ere the Shepherd could bring him back."

He moved into his house and shut the door. But it was too late. The image of the bleeding Shepherd, searching for one lost, stubborn lamb, was imprinted on his mind.

Two weeks later Caldwell attended a small prayer meeting at a school near his home. He told of hearing a song about a shepherd when Mr. Moody had preached to the countryside a few days past. And he asked the believers gathered to pray for him. It was not long before the Shepherd found that lamb and brought him home to stay.

Ira and Moody found their home country was no different from Europe in offering a mixed reception. Skeptical writers on both sides of the ocean found ample material for skewering in the songs and services.

Clowns at a circus were reported as having this conversation: "I am rather Moody tonight. How do you feel?" "I feel rather Sankey-monious."

A Boston writer took liberties with the wildly popular "Hold the Fort."

"Hold the forks, the knives are coming," he parodied, all the way to the end: "Shout the chorus to your neighbor, sling the hash this way."

That particular song even made its way into politics. "Hold the fort for Hayes and Wheeler," supporters shouted in 1876 and 1877 as an election dispute over electoral votes turned into a legal battle. The Compromise of 1877 brought Rutherford B. Hayes into the White House.

Perhaps it's no surprise the songs were borrowed and adapted so often. Many of the tunes Ira sang and wrote were quite simple, allowing people to easily learn the songs and commit the words—and the messages—to heart. Ira continued to put the emphasis on the text.

"You can't do it with music alone," he explained to a Pittsburgh reporter. "You've got to make them hear every word and see every picture of the part."

16
"Hallelujah, 'Tis Done!"

For most of 1876—and then off and on for the next twenty years—Moody and Ira traveled the United States, holding meetings like those that had so stirred Britain. Even in the great cities, it sometimes was impossible to find a meeting place large enough to hold the crowds that surged in to hear Mr. Moody preach the gospel and Mr. Sankey sing it.

At an early morning meeting in Brooklyn, Ira was astonished to find the five-thousand-seat hall packed and many more people being turned away. He was told that fifteen thousand were sent home for want of seats in the afternoon.

The masses brought with them particular cares and blessings. It was not uncommon for a noon meeting to include the reading of two hundred or three hundred prayer requests. It also was not uncommon for Ira to have a choir of two hundred and fifty or more join him to help lead the singing and prepare hearts to respond submissively to the Savior.

Despite the vast numbers, Ira tried to keep his attention fixed on individual souls in need. He loved to work in the inquiry room after a meeting, pulling aside men with broken hearts and pointing them to Christ.

One young man left a deep impression. Ira caught his eye as he entered the room and beckoned him over.

"Good evening, sir," Ira said. "I am so glad you have answered the prodding on your heart. Have you come to accept Christ as your Savior?"

"I would gladly accept Him, but I know He won't accept me," the young man said.

"Why do you say that?" Ira asked.

"I have been an infidel for many years, sir, and have privately and publicly taken every opportunity to speak against Christ. I have traveled the world in my mission to defy Him. Do you still wonder why I doubt He would forgive me?"

Anguish was in the man's voice and his body shook with it.

"Do you want Him to forgive you?" Ira asked.

"I don't know," the young man said. "I don't know what's the matter with me. I don't know why I'm here tonight. I don't know why I came to this room. I haven't been myself for two days, and I can't understand why. I only know I'm desperately unhappy."

Ira prayed for wisdom as he spoke again.

"My dear friend, what you need tonight is Christ," Ira said. "He will dispel your gloom and sorrow and bring clarity to your confusion. 'Seek and ye shall find' is His promise to you, right there in the book of Luke."

"But I have fought against Him my whole life. And I believed I was right. Perhaps I still believe it!"

"Then why are you here?" Ira asked quietly.

"I don't know," the young man said. "I have not been inside a church in eight years or spoken to a Christian in that time either."

He cupped his head in his hands. Ira let the silence stand, certain the young man had more to say. He was right.

"About a year ago, I received a letter from my poor old mother, away over in Dundee, Scotland. She asked me to make her one promise, that when Mr. Moody and Mr. Sankey came back to America I would go to hear them.

"I told her I would, and here I am. I have come two nights, and I have had not one minute's peace since the first night. And now here I am, talking to you."

"Young man, this is the answer to your mother's prayers," Ira said. "What do we know but that she's praying at this very moment? Do not delay. The Savior is surely calling you and to resist would be foolhardy. Yield to Him. He will receive you."

The young man lowered his head again. Ira could see him struggling physically as he must have been struggling spiritually. Then, suddenly, the man grabbed his hand.

"By the grace of God, I take Jesus Christ as my Savior now!"

Ira clapped him on the back, and they prayed together, Ira joyful and the young man finally peaceful.

They met again a few nights later at the door into the hall.

"My friend!" Ira said. "Have you written to your mother?"

"A letter is on the way," he said. "But I could not wait. I sent her a cable that very night."

"And what did it say?"

"I've found Jesus."

"Thank the Lord!" Ira said.

"Yes," the young man answered, "and that is just what my mother answered me."

From New York to Philadelphia, Chicago to Boston, Moody led a growing team of preachers and laymen who ministered to people almost all day long in each city. Thousands came in each place, and when the meetings ended, hundreds or even thousands had publicly confessed Christ.

The rolls of visitors included great and notorious men—President Ulysses S. Grant, the writer Samuel Clemens, and P. T. Barnum, already well known by then for his shocking displays of the strange and for his traveling circus, which he had begun calling "The Greatest Show on Earth." The meetings drew curious Mormons in Salt Lake City and, at Moody's personal invitation, black Christians in Chattanooga, Tennessee.

Ira never tired of the endless train trips. He loved engaging his fellow passengers on the news of the day and was not afraid of topics that others avoided.

On one trip from Chicago to New York, having covered the weather easily and come across no difficulty with politics, he broached religion with his seatmate. The conversation found its way to the evangelistic efforts of Mr. Moody and his colleague Mr. Sankey.

"I never had the pleasure of hearing either of them, though, of course, I've heard much of them," the stranger said.

Ira, in a light mood, answered solemnly, though he struggled to keep his voice from betraying him.

"Ah, I have had occasion to hear both men, more than once."

"Indeed? What kind of folks are they?"

"Oh, just common folks like you and me," Ira said.

The other man turned in his seat to face Ira more directly and lowered his voice just a bit.

"My daughter plays the organ—we have a small one at home—and the whole family very much enjoys singing from Mr. Sankey's *Gospel Hymns*. I regret I never had the chance to hear him sing 'The Ninety and Nine' before he died."

Ira did not try to hide his shock.

"Died? How do you know he died? I have heard no such thing."

"Oh, yes, it's true. I read in the paper not a week or two past," the stranger said.

"Well," Ira said, "it must be true if you have seen it in the papers."

The whistle blew then, and the man looked out to see his stop approaching as the train slowed.

"I've enjoyed our visit," he said. "I hope the rest of your journey is pleasant."

He stepped into the aisle and reached for his bag, but Ira stopped him.

"Wait, please. I hardly think it is fair that we should part without me telling you that I am one of the men we have been talking about."

"What? Who are you?"

"I am what is left of Sankey."

The man grabbed his bag quickly and gave Ira a confused look.

"Well. What a strange jester you are. But you can't play that on me, old fellow. Sankey is dead."

He turned quickly and was gone. Ira sat back into his seat and pressed his lips together to hold in a laugh.

17

"My Help Comes from the Lord of Hosts"

Besides crossing and re-crossing the United States, Moody and Ira traveled several more times to Great Britain.

Each time they arrived, Ira would shake his head in amazement, recalling that first trip when they had been much younger men with no invitation but from the dead. Now they were met by crowds, and those crowds included brothers and sisters who had been reached by the gospel during earlier campaigns.

Moody never tired of greeting these people, treating each as a dear old friend. When the services ended and inquiry rooms finally quieted, he would stay on until every hand had been shaken, every story of a changed life told.

Ira, however, was wearing out. For their 1891 trip to the United Kingdom, they planned to visit ninety-nine towns in ninety days with as many as three meetings scheduled in each town.

Ira began with enthusiasm but was forced to return early to the States, his voice and his body equally exhausted. His doctor suggested a real rest, a getaway to some place enjoyable, some place he would not sing.

It took time—years, in fact—to convince Ira of the need and then to make the plans, but finally, in 1898, Ira and Fanny, along with other family members and friends, journeyed to the Holy Land. Ira was nearly sixty but his enthusiasm at the prospect of all he was about to see made him seem much younger.

They began their explorations in Egypt: Cairo, the great pyramids, the Nile.

Ira took in all the usual tourist sites but also couldn't pass up the chance to learn how the gospel fared in this country. In Cairo he visited the American Mission and found the church filled with his own countrymen as well as Egyptians and Englishmen.

He entered late, slipped into a seat, and directed his attention to the speaker. Moments later, the man sitting beside him leaned in.

"Are you not Mr. Sankey?" he whispered.

Ira nodded politely and smiled, then turned back to the speaker. But his neighbor was not put off.

"What a pleasure, sir. I do hope we shall convince you to sing for us when the message is done."

Ira turned to face the man again.

"I have come here for rest, my friend," he whispered.

The other man's smile faltered. Ira hesitated only a moment before speaking again: "However, it is no strain for me to sing of my Savior, no matter the stated purpose of my journey."

He looked around, his eyes quickly covering the space at the front of the building.

"I don't see an organ or piano though. It would be hard for me to sing without being able to accompany myself."

The other man looked too.

"Ah," he said. "I had not thought of that. Well, thank you, anyway."

Ira smiled again, and they both turned their attention back to the front.

Minutes later Ira heard a hushed female voice near his right ear.

"Mr. Sankey? It is Mr. Sankey, is it not? What a surprise, sir, what a delightful surprise. I do hope you will sing for us when the service has ended."

Ira turned and quietly explained that the question had already been settled by the absence of an instrument. This new friend—a fellow Pennsylvanian, she told him—was not so easily deterred as his first inquirer.

She slipped from her row and spoke in a low voice to four Egyptian soldiers.

Ira was astonished a few minutes later to see those same four men return, carrying a small cabinet organ onto the platform where they settled it quietly. The speaker turned for a moment to see what was causing the stir in the crowd, and then returned to his address.

Ira began to mentally prepare a song list.

When the speaker had finished, Ira was introduced by the missionary who had first asked him to sing.

"My friends, we have with us tonight an esteemed visitor, one of whom I know you've all heard. Mr. Ira Sankey, will you come, please, and sing the gospel to us as we know you can?"

Ira sang for a half hour and then sang more when the crowd pressed him. Finally, his voice weary but his heart light, he said he would close with "Saved by Grace."

It was one of his personal favorites, with a text by his friend, Fanny Crosby.

"Some day the silver cord will break, and I no more as now shall sing; but, oh, the joy when I shall wake within the palace of the King!"

Ira could not sing the chorus without remembering his friend's sightless eyes and without regretting the many days when he did not share her fervor to see her Savior. "And I shall see Him face to face and tell the story—saved by grace."

He sang many more times as he traveled through Egypt and into the Holy Land, where he explored cities such as Bethlehem, Jericho, and Bethany. His emotions often surprised him in this strange, exotic land, and not only when he sang. When he saw these places, it was impossible not to feel closer to the One who had walked them.

In Jerusalem he rose early one morning to walk a short distance from their hotel to the Tower of David.

The tower was built long after David's reign. But as a focal point in his city, it came to bear his name. It was part of a larger, fortresslike complex near Jerusalem's Jaffa Gate.

Parts of the citadel had been rebuilt many times as Jerusalem fell into different hands throughout its history. But for more than three hundred years now, its history had been peaceful. The actual tower that Ira planned to scale was built in 1655. The citadel had been serving since that time as a garrison for Turkish troops. Ira cared nothing for the Ottoman Empire's military regime, but he longed to climb that tower and get a broader view of Jerusalem, imagining as he did what it might have looked like when King David himself looked upon it.

He met a guard at the base of the stairs and without using any common words between them, the two managed to convey to each other that Ira wanted to climb the tower and that the guard would not let him do any such thing without some sort of special permission.

Ira studied the man's face closely for a moment, and then pulled a few coins from the small purse in his pocket. His permit secured, he found himself moments later climbing the winding stairs with another armed guard close behind him.

The spectacle was all Ira had imagined and more. He could see the full outline of the citadel, its ancient walls and the lines where newer ones joined to them. He could see the green wilderness beyond the walls and imagined sheep on the hills.

Ira glanced at his companion to see if his time was running short. The man would not meet his eye. Ira turned back to the view and searched his mind. His trusty notebook was back in the hotel, but he had no need of it. Psalm 121 was just the thing.

"I to the hills will—" he began to sing.

The guard rushed at him, alarm in his eyes. Ira smiled around his words and kept singing.

"—lift mine eyes, from whence my help doth come. my help comes from the Lord of hosts, which hath made heav'n and earth."

The guard stood just beside him but made no move to stop him. And when Ira finished, letting the final G of the tune "Belmont" ring over the waking city, the other man smiled and tipped his hat.

Ira continued to Constantinople and Rome. Everywhere he met people singing his songs and everywhere he sang too.

After a trip that few physicians would have considered restful, it was back to England and back to work. Ira visited thirty cities, singing and telling stories of the gospel songs that people so loved to hear. But he found the schedule more exhausting than it had been twenty years before. His spirit for the work grew stronger by the year, but his body was on the opposite course.

18

"No Dark Valley when Jesus Comes to Gather His Loved Ones Home"

Moody and Ira had worked closely for more than a quarter of a century. For many of those years, they were scarcely separated.

But as they aged, the men pursued some separate ministries. They traveled apart more often and were busy with the projects dear to their hearts: Moody, his schools, and Ira, his sacred song services.

Ira's songbook had gone all over the world by now. And as people sang and listened to the words of the songs, many yielded to the Holy Spirit. Afterward they often would write to Ira, telling how the songs had touched their hearts. Others came to him when a service ended to say they wouldn't be there had they not heard one of his songs and surrendered to the Lord so many years before.

Ira loved these stories and found that others did too. As Moody became more involved at Northfield, Ira devoted his time to preparing a special program of songs and stories. He would sing the pieces that had become favorites and intersperse them with stories of lives changed and hearts restored to fellowship with their Maker.

But even as they pursued separate interests, the two men continued periodically to reunite for services throughout the United States.

In fall 1899, they were together in Brooklyn, where Ira now resided. Moody spoke from John 11, highlighting the love of Christ through the story of Mary, Martha, and Lazarus. He was intense and emotional, as usual.

"He is as powerful a speaker today as he was the day I met him," Ira said to Dr. Storr, the pastor of the church.

Storr nodded.

"He has the power of God on him, no doubt of that," he said. "I am thankful we planned this meeting well in advance. Do you know he already has most of his calendar filled for next year?"

Ira didn't have a chance to speak privately with Moody that night or the next. And they went their separate ways again. But a few weeks later, walking back to their lodgings after ministering in another church, he told his friend what Storr had said.

"Mr. Moody, I think you should slow down a bit," Ira said. "Do you really have so many meetings planned already?"

Moody smiled.

"I think our friend was exaggerating a bit, Ira. But I do have a fair number of meetings scheduled. I believe you're right—better to stop saying yes now than to make plans I'll have to cancel."

They walked in companionable silence the few blocks to their hotel.

"We're not the men we used to be, Ira," Moody said as he grasped the railing to climb the stairs to the front door. He was smiling again.

"Well, sir, speak on your own behalf. I for one would be happy to sail again to England tomorrow—if only I could have someone along to read my newspaper to me and collect my clippings and answer letters."

"There," Moody said. "You make my very point. You may have the heart of the man you used to be, but you have not his eyes!"

They both laughed.

"Good night, Ira."

"Good night, Mr. Moody."

Ira went to Canada and returned just before Christmas to find a letter from Moody waiting. It was nine pages long and full of tales of the work in Chicago and Northfield while Ira was away.

"The children prosper under the discipline and love of their teachers," Moody wrote. "I am gladdened beyond words to see them at their studies and hear them give testimony of Christ's work in their lives. But enough of my projects. We must speak now of our next meeting. I am to arrive back in New York on Wednesday. Can you meet me at the Murray Hill Hotel? We can discuss our plans for these next services."

But shortly after writing the letter, Moody collapsed in Kansas City. His son William was called to bring his father home to Northfield.

Ira received frequent letters, sometimes daily, with updates on his friend's health. In mid-December, he traveled to Northfield to pay a visit. Moody's wife, Emma, met him on the front porch, a shawl wrapped tightly around her slumped shoulders. She looked weary, Ira thought.

"What is the news today, Mrs. Moody?" he said.

"Oh, Ira, I'm glad you've come. He's poorly today, I'm afraid, but I hope he'll be able to see you in a while. Come in and get warm."

The Moody children all were there. Ira smiled to see three generations cuddled together near the fire: Moody's wife, Emma; his daughter, Emma; and his granddaughter, also Emma. The daughter was the image of her mother when Ira had first met her. And the granddaughter clearly was on the path to the same sweet face.

Paul was home from Yale. He had been the last to come, since his mother urged him to complete his exams before leaving for the Christmas break and what she believed would be his last visits with his father.

William, the eldest, lived at Northfield and visited daily. Ira grieved to see his care-worn face that afternoon. William had lost a son and a daughter in the past two years. It seemed certain he soon would bid his father farewell too.

"How is the little one?" Ira asked William.

It was the right question. William's eyes brightened.

"He is well, thank you, Mr. Sankey," he said. "I do not know another child of six weeks so sweet-tempered and easily pleased. My wife is not half worn out caring for him and is even able to enjoy many quiet moments with him. We praise God for this."

"Indeed," Ira said, "a blessing and a kindness for ones He has asked to bear so much."

"Thank you, sir," William said.

Ira stayed the night, but Moody did not improve. In the morning Ira bundled himself against the cold, shook hands with William and Paul, and pressed Emma's hand between both of his.

"I will be back soon," he said. "Will you tell him I was here, when he is himself again?"

Ira was home in Brooklyn when the next message came.

"Moody dead at noon. Come promptly."

Fanny read the words to him once and then again. Her hand trembled as she set the slip of paper on the table and reached for Ira's hands.

"I am sorry, Ira," she said. "It is a great loss."

Ira squeezed her hand gently but said nothing. A tear trailed down each cheek and into his beard.

"I would have liked to say farewell to him," he said finally. "I should have spoken to him last week. Had I only known death was so near—"

"There was nothing left unsaid between you two, Ira," Fanny said. She was crying now too. "No last word could have said more than you have said already to each other and to the world."

They had been sitting quietly for an hour or more when they heard a knock at the door. A reporter from the *New York Times* stood on the step, hat in hand.

"My respects and condolences, Mr. Sankey. Would you mind making a brief statement about your esteemed colleague?"

Ira invited the man in and delivered a few of the stories he loved so well. In his element now, his grief became useful as he told the world what it should remember about his friend.

"Mr. Moody was one of the greatest men of this century, in the marvelous common sense he exhibited, in his earnestness in his life work, and in his desire to help people, and to do good," Ira said. "He was the most unselfish man I ever knew."

19

"Within the Palace of the King"

Ira no longer enjoyed the robust health that had carried him through so many decades of travel and ministry. His eyesight was failing, and he was generally worn out and susceptible to every illness to which he was exposed.

But he wasn't done working. His trips were fewer, but Ira was busy at home, putting together the manuscript that had been forming in his head for more than twenty years.

The Story of the Gospel Hymns, he called it.

All those anecdotes he'd been filing in his notebooks— one had long since ceased to be enough—all the letters he and Moody had received, all the transformations he'd seen firsthand he painstakingly recorded, with Fanny at his side acting as assistant and filling in gaps when his memory failed.

The book was nearly finished when Ira and Fanny took a trip to Michigan in 1901. They were guests of Dr. John Harvey Kellogg, visiting his renowned Battle Creek Sanitarium System.

Under Kellogg's management, the facility had grown from a farmhouse assisting a dozen patients with various water treatments to a well-known health resort equipped to host as many as seven hundred guests at a time.

Wealthy and prominent people visited regularly, some for pampering, others for more medically oriented care. Kellogg billed it as a "place where people learn to stay well." Besides medical attention and diagnostics, guests were taught about healthful diets and encouraged to exercise. Ira came for rest and rejuvenation. Instead, for the second time in his life, he felt the fury of fire and experienced its devastation. On February 18, 1902, the main building and the hospital were consumed. Most of the guests saved their lives and nothing more. Ira was among them. And among the belongings he could not save was his manuscript.

The loss discouraged him more than anything in many years. He had loved the stories like old friends and had delighted in the prospect of sharing them.

"You can write it again, Ira," Fanny said as they sat before the fire in a hotel room that night.

Ira did not answer her. His face seemed to sag, contrasting sharply with the crisp, new, ill-fitting suit he wore. They had been all over town that afternoon, replacing the things they would need immediately and making arrangements to have other things sent from New York.

"There is time," Fanny said. "You have plenty of time. I will help you."

Again, silence. The fire snapped and hissed.

"I think it's best this way, Fanny," Ira said finally. "Perhaps I had lost sight of the Savior and put too much of Ira Sankey in those pages."

"No, Ira, you hadn't. You are too careful for that. Those stories told people about your God and His work. Those stories need to be told, and you can still tell them."

Ira looked at her then.

"Fanny, you, of all people, know the hours I've spent on that book. You know how I've labored over it. I can't imagine starting again from nothing."

"Not nothing, Ira. We have so much still, so many letters at home, and your notebooks. You simply need to reorganize and tell it again. It will be better, perhaps, in the retelling. Who knows?"

He smiled, just a little.

"My Fanny," he said. "Where would I be without you?"

"Well, I don't know that you'd try many new things or risk any grand adventures," she said, laughing. "I only wish Mr. Moody was here to help me convince you."

"I never could withstand the absolute conviction of the two of you that a thing could be done."

"He'd side with me, I know," Fanny said.

"Let's get some rest," Ira answered.

Fanny's was only the first urging. Many other friends and colleagues took up the same cry, and Ira was soon back at the book. But he couldn't remember or find all the materials he'd started with, and the manuscript seemed, to him, thin.

Worse, he struggled mightily to read his notes and the letters he'd kept for years in boxes and files. He strained and turned to find the best light. His eyes throbbed and ached after even short periods of work.

In early 1903 he was forced to set his writing aside and seek help for his failing eyesight.

Dr. Richard Kalish prescribed surgery to relieve the intense pain Ira was experiencing from congestive glaucoma. The procedure did ease his pain, but his sight did not return as he healed.

As she had so many times, Fanny stepped in to bolster her husband's weary spirit.

She read him his morning newspaper over breakfast, his letters around noon, and his afternoon paper when they had finished their walk around the block, Ira shuffling slightly and Fanny gripping his elbow firmly.

During these dark days, an old friendship took on a new, deeper meaning to him.

Ira liked to ask Fanny Crosby each time they met what she had prepared for an emergency. It was a reminder of the day he first heard one of her dearest-loved songs, "Saved by Grace."

It was back in 1894, and Moody was traveling in England again. Ira had remained in the States and was assisting A. J. Gordon in services at Northfield. Crosby was in attendance.

"We've had several requests to hear from you, Fanny," he said.

"Oh, no, Mr. Sankey, I cannot, I have nothing to say, I am not prepared."

Ira and Gordon urged her to speak her heart, and Gordon gave the final plea she could not refuse.

"Fanny, do you speak to please man or to please God?" he said.

"Why, I hope to please God."

"Well then, go out and do your duty."

The logic was not impeccable, but Crosby felt she must respond.

She spoke briefly of her life and work.

"I would like to tell you why I write," she said. "I find the words pouring from my heart as I consider what awaits me.

"Some day the silver cord will break, and I no more as now shall sing; but oh, the joy when I shall wake within the palace of the King! And I shall see Him face to face, and tell the story—saved by grace."

See Him. Ira wondered when he would stop being surprised by how often his blind friend spoke of sight.

When Crosby returned to her seat, he hurried to her.

"I've not heard that before," Ira said. "Where have you kept that piece?"

"Oh, I wrote it some years ago."

"What?"

"I've been saving it for an emergency," she said.

Ira could scarcely contain his laughter.

Now as she arrived for the first time since he'd lost his own sight, the old question hung in the air. Fanny Sankey helped their visitor settle into a comfortable chair near the fire. Ira spent many days in bed, but he had risen and dressed this morning. He would receive their friend properly, he told his wife.

Crosby easily slipped into the chair to which Fanny directed her. Ira, who stood when she came in, was a long moment backing his calves into another chair, lowering himself warily, and then trying to adjust the chair so it faced her voice.

"I am sorry to find you so, Ira," said Crosby, who was recently widowed.

"And have you anything prepared for an emergency such as this?" he asked.

Fanny Sankey smiled broadly, though neither of her companions saw it.

"It is so good of you to come, Fanny," she said. "You have been on our hearts these past months."

Until recently Crosby had been living in Brooklyn, not far from Ira and Fanny. But in June 1902, her husband died. She moved to Connecticut, where she lived with her widowed sister.

"We are all a great deal closer to heaven than we were as new friends, aren't we?" Crosby said. "Well, we have

sung of it for years, and I for one am not sorry to see the
time quickly approaching."

They shared a light meal and lighter memories. Then
Crosby returned to their first topic.

"I believe the entire Christian world is praying for your
recovery, Ira," she said. "I hear it everywhere. The papers
and quarterlies all overflow with wishes for your health
and your next meetings to be scheduled."

"Well, when you speak to the world, you may say that
I am holding on to Christ and Christ is holding on to
me," Ira said. "By and by I'll see him face to face and tell
the story saved by grace."

"I am eager for that day myself," Crosby said.

Fanny Sankey was smiling again, but this time her un-
seen face also wore tears. Crosby spoke again.

"Tell me," she said, "will I be reading that book of
yours any time soon?"

"Oh, to have both of you after me like some naughty
schoolboy," Ira said.

"Does that mean you're not working on it?"

"It is not that I *am* not, my friend. I *cannot*. Too many
stories were in my files that went up with the manuscript.
Too much is lost."

"He sounds like the Ira who left Chicago," Fanny
Sankey said. "Nothing left, no ministry left, impossible
to begin again. I tell him over and over he must simply
have needed a fresh start and our Lord provided it."

"Well, it felt so good to finish my first, I'm already at
work on another," Crosby said. "Don't let this pass, Ira.
You have stories people want to hear, stories they need
to hear."

Whether it was the urging of friends or his own heart
that swung the decision, Ira did get back to the book.
His own life story was not so difficult to retell. In fact,
he fancied it was better the second time, with fewer

Ira Sankey

unnecessary details. But the stories of the songs, those were not so easy. He was determined to tell them well and accurately—he had no use for his own memory as the agent of facts.

Considering Ira had always turned to the newspapers for information, it is strange the idea had to come from Fanny. At her urging, he composed a short letter and sent it to the *New York Times*.

On Oct. 7, 1905, the *Times*' Saturday Review of Books carried this item:

"Mr. Ira D. Sankey, formerly associated with the late Dwight L. Moody in evangelical work, informs us that he is rewriting his unpublished book, *The Story of the Gospel Hymns*, the original manuscript of which was destroyed by fire four years ago, and asks us to give space to his request that our readers will acquaint him with any facts or anecdotes they may have touching the modern hymns. Mr. Sankey's address is 148 S. Oxford St., Brooklyn Borough."

The letters came. More stories, perhaps, than he had even collected the first time, in a lifetime of saving.

Ira finished his book for the second time and held a copy in his hands two years before his death. He could not read it for himself, but he listened with pleasure to his own retellings of the life-changing impact of those songs he loved so well.

Ira and Fanny were often alone now. Many friends wished to visit, but most were turned away. Ira was tired and Fanny too consumed with him to spend time entertaining others.

But the occasional guest was welcomed.

At a quiet dinner one old friend noted how changed Ira's life was from the days when he was always in a throng, always answering a question or telling another story.

"Does the Holy Spirit seem as strong to you now as in those days of service?" he asked.

"Stronger," Ira answered. "More powerful. Then, there were so many distractions. God and I are together most of the time now."

On August 13, 1908, the last distractions were left behind, and Ira went home to his Savior. The *New York Times* reported he was faintly singing Crosby's song as he died: "But oh, the joy when I shall wake within the palace of the King!"

EPILOGUE

"Yes, I'll Sing the Wondrous Story"

Throughout his lifetime, newspaper critics declared Ira to be flat on high notes and pointed out—sometimes snidely—that his was obviously an untrained voice. But few seem to have questioned his commitment to the message. His half-sung, half-spoken style always centered on one goal: Communicating the gospel.

In 1894, Ira tried to explain his philosophy to a reporter from the *Pittsburgh Leader*. He said music alone was insufficient to pierce the soul, and his listeners must hear every word he sang.

"Then you'll get that silence of death, that quiet before God," he said.

Ira never claimed to be a great singer. In fact, Moody was known to emphasize the work of God in their ministry by saying there were certainly men who could preach better than he and others who could sing better than Ira.

But a Moody biographer, writing in the 1930s, estimated that four of every six people who came to the meetings came to hear Sankey sing and to sing along with him the "catchy, easily-learned, easily-vocalized airs and choruses which constituted the musical part of the services."

His gift was not song but spirit, said Robert Boyd, in his 1875 book about Moody and Ira's ministry.

George C. Stebbins agreed. He wrote of his friend: "He demonstrated, in a most remarkable way . . . the power of the individual singer of the gospel, so that it has become a great ministry in evangelism."

Bibliography

Crosby, Fanny. *Fanny Crosby's Life Story.* New York: Every Where Publishing Co., 1903.

Everett, Betty Steele. *Ira Sankey: First Gospel Singer.* Fort Washington, PA: Christian Literature Crusade, 1999.

Goodspeed, Rev. E.J. *A Full History of the Wonderful Career of Moody and Sankey in Great Britain and America.* New York: Henry S. Goodspeed & Co., 1876.

Lobb, John. *Arrows and Anecdotes.* London: Christian Age Office, 1876.

McPherson, James. *The Battle Cry of Freedom.* New York: Oxford University Press, 2003.

Murphy, Jim. *The Great Fire.* New York: Scholastic, Inc., 1995.

Rothwell, Helen. *Sankey: The Singer and His Song.* 1946. Belfast: Ambassador, 1996.

Sankey, Ira. *My Life and the Story of the Gospel Hymns.* New York: Harper & Brothers, 1906.